HEIRS OF PROMISE

THE CHURCH AS THE NEW ISRAEL IN ROMANS

Also in the Snapshots series:

Transformation: The Heart of Paul's Gospel

by David A. deSilva

For updates on this series, visit LexhamPress.com

HEIRS OF PROMISE

THE CHURCH AS THE NEW ISRAEL IN ROMANS

Snapshots

Michael F. Bird, Series Editor

P. Chase Sears

LEXHAM PRESS

To my wife, who is a true daughter of Sarah (1 Peter 3:6)

Heirs of Promise: The Church as the New Israel in Romans
Snapshots

Copyright 2015 P. Chase Sears

Lexham Press, 1313 Commercial St., Bellingham, WA 98225
LexhamPress.com

Print ISBN 978-1-57-799648-4
Digital ISBN 978-1-57-799649-1

Series Editor: Michael F. Bird
Lexham Editorial Team: David Bomar, Abigail Stocker
Cover Design: Christine Gerhart
Back Cover Design: Brittany VanErem
Typesetting: ProjectLuz.com

TABLE OF CONTENTS

ABBREVIATIONS

1QH^a	*Hodayot*ᵃ, or *Thanksgiving Hymns*ᵃ
1QS	*Serek hayyaad,* or *Rule of the Community*
4QFlor	*Florilegium* (4Q174)
4QAramaic Apocalypse	"Son of God" Text (4Q246)
Ant.	*Jewish Antiquities*
As. Mos.	*Assumption of Moses*
1 Enoch	*1 (Ethiopic) Enoch*
4 Ezra	*4 Ezra*
Jdt	Judith
Jub.	*Jubilees*
1–4 Macc	1–4 Maccabees
Pss. Sol.	*Psalms of Solomon*
Sobr.	*On Sobriety*
T. Sim.	*Testament of Simeon*
Tob	Tobit
Wis	Wisdom of Solomon

CHAPTER 1

Introduction

The relationship between the Church and Israel is an intriguing subject and one that has significant implications for how Christians understand the fulfillment of Old Testament promises. This issue is one that even the earliest of Christians wrestled with as Gentiles began to hear and believe the gospel of Jesus Christ (Acts 11:1–18). For example, the question arose as to whether Gentiles should be required to adopt Jewish identification markers, including circumcision (Acts 15:1–21). In answering this question, the apostles declared that God has made no distinction between Jews and Gentiles. As a result of this declaration, they did not require the Gentiles to become ethnically Jewish in order to join the people of God (Acts 15:7–9). Later, as the early church expanded through the ministry of Paul, the once-predominately Jewish church became overwhelmingly Gentile. This transformation then presented new questions, questions concerning whether God had abandoned the nation of Israel (Rom 9–11).

As such questions surfaced concerning the place of believing Jews and Gentiles in the people of God, the apostles explained this new relationship in light of the fulfillment of the OT promises made to Israel (Gal 4:28; 6:15). These promises consist of a new creation (Isa 42:9; 43:18–19; 48:6–7; 65:17; 66:22; cf. Gal 6:15; 2 Cor 5:17), whereby God would deliver his people from exile (Isa 26:19; 40:9; 52:7; 60:6; 61:1; Ezek 37:1–4; cf. Rom 10), establishing a new covenant with them (Jer 31:31ff; Ezek 36:22–26; cf. Eph 2:18–22; 2 Cor 3:4–6; Heb 8:1–13) and, thus, fulfilling God's promise to Abraham that in him all the nations would be blessed (Gen 12:1–3; 15:4–5; 17:1–8; 18:18–19; 22:16–18; cf. Rom 4; Gal 3:1–9).

Though a complicated subject among first-century Christians, the majority of the church throughout history has concluded that the NT teaches that the fulfillment of these OT promises to Israel is to be found in the Church. In the second century, Justin Martyr explained to a Jew named Trypho that Christians are "the true spiritual Israel, and descendants of Judah, Jacob, Isaac, and Abraham."[1] Augustine held a similar idea, saying, "For if we hold with a firm heart the grace of God which hath been given us, we are Israel, the seed of Abraham. ... Let therefore no Christian consider himself alien to the name of Israel."[2] Among the Reformers, such as Luther and Calvin, it was also believed that the Church was true Israel.[3] This view has even been expressed by modern theo-

1. Justin Martyr, "Dialogue of Justin with Trypho, a Jew," in *The Apostolic Fathers with Justin Martyr and Irenaeus*, ed. Alexander Roberts, James Donaldson, and A. Cleveland Coxe, vol. 1, The Ante-Nicene Fathers (Buffalo, NY: Christian Literature Company, 1885), 200.

2. Philip Schaff, ed., *Saint Augustine: Expositions on the Book of Psalms*, vol. 8, A Select Library of the Nicene and Post-Nicene Fathers of the Christian Church, First Series (New York: Christian Literature Company, 1880), 550.

3. Martin Luther, *Galatians*, Crossway Classic Commentaries (Wheaton, IL: Crossway Books, 1998), 303; John Calvin, *Commentaries on the Epistles of Paul to the Galatians and Ephesians* (Bellingham, WA: Logos Bible Software, 2010), 186.

logians like Karl Barth, who saw the Church as the successor of Israel.[4]

However, despite this longstanding history, both dispensational and post-Holocaust theologians have recently challenged the idea that the Church is the new Israel.[5] The former maintain that many of the promises made to OT Israel still find their ultimate fulfillment in a future national restoration rather than in the Church.[6] The latter oppose the idea that the promises to OT Israel are fulfilled in the Church for fear that such a concession has contributed to anti-Semitism.[7] In light

---

4. Karl Barth, *Church Dogmatics: The Doctrine of God*, vol. 2.2 (London: T&T Clark, 1957), 201.

5. Dispensationalism is a system of interpreting the Bible developed in the 19th century that emphasizes God's particular dealings (dispensations) with humanity throughout history. Although it has taken several forms (see below), the common denominator among all forms of dispensationalism is a "belief in a future restoration of national Israel" (Michael J. Vlach, *Has the Church Replaced Israel?: A Theological Evaluation* [Nashville: B&H Academic, 2010], 72n55). "Post-Holocaust theology" is a term used to describe a reactionary movement that sees one of the major contributors to the Holocaust to be the anti-Judaism teaching of some forms of Christianity. From this perspective, anti-Judaism is any attempt to define Christianity "as over and against Judaism, better than Judaism, as a new, superior, gentile, and universal people with a better religion and a better God ... [and is] simply ... another form of idolatry and oppression that a true witness to the God of Israel must always resist" (Clark M. Williamson, *A Guest in the House of Israel: Post-Holocaust Church Theology* [Westminster John Knox Press, 1993], 250.). Some post-Holocaust theologians suggest that the church has no mission to evangelize Jews (ibid.; Susan Eastman, "Israel and the Mercy of God: A Re-Reading of Galatians 6.16 and Romans 9–11," *New Testament Studies* 56 [2010]: 394).

6. See Barry E. Horner, *Future Israel: Why Christian Anti-Judaism Must Be Challenged* (Nashville: B&H Academic, 2007), 232–34; Vlach, *Has the Church Replaced Israel*, 161–62; J. Lanier Burns, "The Future of Ethnic Israel in Romans 11," in *Dispensationalism, Israel, and the Church: The Search for Definition* (Grand Rapids: Zondervan, 1992), 188–229.

7. See Richard H. Bell, *The Irrevocable Call of God: An Inquiry into Paul's Theology of Israel*, Wissenschaftliche Untersuchungen zum Neuen Testament 184 (Tübingen: Mohr Siebeck, 2005), 408–22. It is fascinating to note that some dispensationalists have joined in making similar arguments, asserting that the belief that the Church is the new or true Israel is a major cause for anti-Semitism throughout the years (see Horner, *Future Israel*, viii–ix).

of these challenges, it will prove helpful to highlight the key areas of disagreement.

FRAMING THE DEBATE

Among evangelicals, the discussion concerning the relationship between the Church and Israel has primarily concentrated on how the NT explains the fulfillment of OT promises. For instance, do the promises given to OT Israel find their fulfillment in the Church? Or does ethnic Israel retain particular promises distinct from believing Gentiles? How one answers these questions will certainly affect his or her approach to interpreting Scripture.

Dispensationalism

Dispensational theologians have answered these questions in various ways, but all maintain some unique privilege for ethnic Israel in the future. However, it is helpful to be aware of some key differences between dispensationalists. "Classical dispensationalism" is represented by the writings of John Nelson Darby and Lewis Sperry Chafer. At the heart of classical dispensationalism is the notion that God has two distinct redemptive purposes for Israel and the Church. For Israel, God will fulfill his purposes with it as the earthly people of God, whereby it will reign over the Gentiles forever in God's kingdom on earth. The Church, on the other hand, is the heavenly people, who will dwell forever in God's kingdom in heaven.[8] Consequently, classical dispensationalists believe that the Church and Israel will be eternally separated.

---

8. Craig A. Blaising and Darrell L. Bock, *Progressive Dispensationalism* (Grand Rapids: Baker Books, 1993), 23–30.

"Revised dispensationalism," advocated by the likes of Charles Ryrie and John Walvoord, veered away from the eternal dualism between the Church and Israel. However, a sharp distinction between the two was still preserved.[9] Revised dispensationalists believe that God is still accomplishing his plan to redeem a people for himself, but the promises of the kingdom in the OT have been put on pause until God's purposes in the Church are complete. It will be at this time that God will resume his plan with Israel, and it will receive the promised kingdom. Although Israel and the Church will not be eternally separated as earthly people and heavenly people, there will remain a distinction in identity.[10]

In a third variation, "progressive dispensationalism," the Church is no longer viewed as a parenthesis in God's plan. Instead, the Church shares with Israel in God's kingdom purposes and is a part of the one people of God. However, within the "one" people of God,

> Israel retains its Old Testament meaning as an ethnic people throughout the New Testament. Even though the believers in the Church have come to share in the present messianic salvation along with Jews and the Church is now serving God's kingdom purpose, Israel in its historic meaning will yet fulfill its promised destiny.[11]

---

9. Charles Ryrie, *Dispensationalism* (Chicago: Moody Press, 2007), 165–66.
10. Blaising and Bock, *Progressive Dispensationalism*, 32.
11. Robert L. Saucy, *The Case for Progressive Dispensationalism: The Interface Between Dispensational & Non-Dispensational Theology* (Grand Rapids: Zondervan, 1993), 188.

In other words, though the Church is closely related to Israel, progressive dispensationalists still expect the nation of Israel to be restored and to fulfill a future role distinctly privileged over Gentile believers. Supporters of this view include Robert Saucy, Craig Blaising, and Darrell Bock.

Non-Dispensationalism

Non-dispensational theologians see more continuity between the Church and Israel. Through the use of typology, some non-dispensationalists have an almost one-to-one equation between OT Israel and the Church. With this particular approach, "the Church existed in the old dispensation as well as in the new, and was *essentially* the same in both."[12] Such an articulation of the relationship between the Church and Israel has left non-dispensationalists open to the charge of supersessionism.[13] However, some non-dispensationalists have revisited this issue seeking to explain the Bible's teaching on this matter in a more nuanced way.[14] Following this nuanced explanation, the Church is not so much a replacement of Israel as a continuation or expansion of Israel to include the Gentiles. In Christ the division between Jew and Gentile has been removed, thereby bringing believing Gentiles into full membership within the covenant community.

Even with its recognition of greater continuity between Israel and the Church, this view has not precluded some

---

12. Louis Berkhof, *Systematic Theology* (Grand Rapids: Eerdmans, 1938), 571.
13. Vlach, *Has the Church Replaced Israel*, 79. The term "supersessionism" describes the view that the Church has replaced the nation of Israel, leaving the nation with no future purpose in history.
14. Peter J. Gentry and Stephen J. Wellum, *Kingdom through Covenant: A Biblical-Theological Understanding of the Covenants* (Wheaton, IL: Crossway, 2012), 106.

non-dispensationalists from seeing a future salvation for ethnic Israel (Rom 9–11).[15] Nevertheless, these non-dispensationalists who advocate a future salvation for Israel do so differently from progressive dispensationalists, who expect Israel to be "restored to a place of prominence among the nations ... [with a] rebuilt temple in Jerusalem."[16] This difference brings to light what is really at the heart of the debate. The current discussion is not whether the Church has replaced Israel; non-dispensationalists are not arguing this. Rather, the issue is whether believing Gentiles are on equal footing with believing Jews, receiving all OT promises through faith in Christ[17]—it is on *this* point that further dialogue needs to occur.

A BIBLICAL-THEOLOGICAL APPROACH

To further this conversation, I suggest a biblical-theological approach to the topic of whether or not believing Gentiles are on equal footing with believing Jews. My reason: As theologians have debated the relationship between the Church and Israel, discussions are often conducted within the discipline of systematic theology. By this, I mean an examination of the biblical text from an atemporal perspective, seeking to answer contemporary questions. This method often isolates primary texts in order to make logical and philosophical connections to argue one's particular theological perspective. Although systematic theology is to be grounded in biblical exegesis, it

---

15. Thomas R. Schreiner, "The Church as the New Israel and the Future of Ethnic Israel in Paul," *Studia Biblica Et Theologica* 13, no. 1 (April 1983): 17–38.
16. Vlach, *Has the Church Replaced Israel*, 140.
17. Vern S. Poythress, *Understanding Dispensationalists*, 2nd ed. (Phillipsburg, NJ: P&R Publishing, 1994), 135.

is difficult—if not impossible—to give a full treatment to the place of each biblical text within its own historical and redemptive context. An overemphasis in systematics can leave a void in understanding the theology of a particular NT author as it pertains to the relationship between the Church and Israel. A failure to grapple with how a whole book or corpus understands this subject can lead to inaccurate conclusions when dealing with isolated texts.

Therefore, further study needs to be done examining the relationship of the Church and Israel in light of the purposes and arguments of individual NT books and authors. For instance, an adequate engagement in this debate must carefully examine how the NT authors—in this case, Paul in Romans—understand the fulfillment of OT promises. Specifically, three main areas need to be explored within the book of Romans: (1) the role of the Messiah as the Davidic king and covenant head of the people of God; (2) the place that the new-creation promises hold in Paul's greater argument; and (3) the basis on which is Paul able to apply titles, originally given to OT Israel, to the Church. A satisfactory means of exploring these three areas requires a biblical-theological approach to the book of Romans.

"Biblical theology" is a term that can connote many different ideas—so it's important to clarify what I mean by a biblical-theological approach before moving forward. Brian Rosner provides a helpful definition of biblical theology as "theological interpretation of Scripture in and for the church. It proceeds with historical and literary sensitivity and seeks to analyse and synthesize the Bible's teaching about God and his relations to the world on its own terms, maintaining sight of the Bible's overarching narrative and Christocentric focus."[18]

There are several important aspects of Rosner's definition that I'd like to highlight. First, biblical theology is exegetically driven, sensitive to the historical, literary, and theological features of the diverse corpora of Scripture, while at the same time conscious of the interrelationship between these documents as a unified whole. Second, biblical theology is concerned with redemptive history, following the development of theological themes and motifs along the biblical timeline. This redemptive historical timeline finds its culmination in the Messiah. Finally, as the first two features are employed, the Bible is understood on its own terms, allowing Scripture to interpret Scripture.

In this book, I will apply biblical theology—as defined above—to Romans. Out of all his letters, Paul's letter to the Romans contains the most comprehensive treatment of his theology. Though not written as a doctrinal treatise per se, Paul does explain his gospel ministry in light of its place in salvation history. In particular, the book of Romans explores the significance of the Gentile inclusion into the people of God within the story of redemption. For this reason, Romans is a prime candidate for understanding how Paul relates the Church and Israel.

Tracing the New Israel Motif in Romans

In approaching this subject through a biblical-theological lens, I will argue that in the book of Romans, Paul views the

---

18. Brian S. Rosner, "Biblical Theology," in *New Dictionary of Biblical Theology* (Downers Grove, IL: InterVarsity Press, 2000), 10 (italics removed from original).

Church as the "new Israel." However, before moving forward, it may prove helpful to clarify the nuance I'm seeking to attain through the use of this title. By calling the Church the *new* Israel I do not mean the *replacement* of Israel, but rather the *continuation of Israel reconstituted in Christ.* Understood this way, Christ is presented as God's *true* Son/Israel, through whom all of God's purposes for Israel and creation are realized. Consequently, through faith in Christ, the Church, consisting of both Jews and Gentiles, becomes God's *new* covenant people and heirs of all of his saving promises. I'm making an important distinction—between Jesus as the *true* Israel and the Church as the *new* Israel. As Gentry and Wellum aptly explain, "in the case of Israel as a typological pattern, Christ is first and foremost its fulfillment and we, as the church, are viewed as the 'Israel of God' only because of our union with Christ. In other words, we as the church, are *not* the antitypical fulfillment of Israel in the first sense; Christ alone fills that role."[19]

With this distinction made, the assertion that the Church is the new Israel is supported by Paul's interpretation of his ministry of gospel proclamation as it relates to salvation history. Specifically, three features of Paul's gospel will be pursued in the following chapters. First, the gospel centers on God's Son, the true Israel (1:3). It is through Jesus and by virtue of his resurrection that the new age has been inaugurated. Consequently, Jesus currently sits on the throne of David as the covenant head of the new Israel (1:3–6). God's people are no longer defined by ethnicity, but rather as those who belong to Jesus (1:6). As the covenant head, Jesus mediates the OT promises to all those who put their faith in him (5:1).

---

19. Gentry and Wellum, *Kingdom Through Covenant*, 106.

Second, Paul's gospel is a fulfillment of the promised deliverance from exile and a new creation spoken by the prophets (1:2; 8:18–25; 10:15; cf. Isa 52:7; 65:17). Throughout Romans, Paul affirms that the blessings of the new creation have invaded the present; this good news is not limited to Jews, but is for everyone who believes (1:16). Because God's redemption has extended to the Gentiles, the promises to Abraham are being fulfilled (4:16–18). The promised Spirit has been poured out, circumcising the hearts of all those who have faith, thus enabling them to keep the law (2:25–29; 8:1–4). Thus, a crucial argument in this book is to show how these promises made to OT Israel are finding their fulfillment in the Church because of its union with Christ.

The third feature of Paul's gospel is that everyone who believes is given the privileged titles and status of Israel. For example, Paul refers to the Church as God's beloved (1:7), saints (1:7), true Jews (2:25–29), children of Abraham (4:1), adopted sons of God (8:14–15), and heirs of the promise (4:13). All these titles were given to OT Israel, and in Romans Paul applies them to all who believe the gospel.

In summary: This book examines the following three themes: (1) God's Son as the true Israel, so that all those united to Jesus find their identity in him; (2) the OT promises made to Israel regarding deliverance from exile and the new creation, both being fulfilled in the Church; and (3) the application of Israelite titles to all those who believe the gospel. After considering these three themes in relation to the Church, the cumulative argument will show that, in the book of Romans, Paul views the Church to be the new Israel, and thus heirs of promise.

CHAPTER 2

Jesus as God's True Son, Israel

Critical to the argument that Paul views the Church as the new Israel in Romans is Paul's assertion that Jesus is the true Israel, through whom the Church finds its identity. To put it another way, Jesus is the antitypical fulfillment of Israel, and the Church, through union with Christ, can be rightfully called the new Israel.[1] Indeed, this theological theme is found in the opening verses of Paul's letter to the Romans (1:1–7).

In 1:1–7 Paul condenses the heart of the letter into one theologically pregnant paragraph. The focus of this salutation is on "the gospel of God," which Paul has been set apart to proclaim (1:1). In an effort to mend tensions between Jewish and Gentile believers, Paul sought to demonstrate the authenticity of the gospel he preached.[2] Specifically, he saw this gospel as

---

1. Peter J. Gentry and Stephen J. Wellum, *Kingdom Through Covenant: A Biblical-Theological Understanding of the Covenants* (Wheaton, IL: Crossway, 2012), 106.
2. Thomas R. Schreiner, *Romans*, Baker Exegetical Commentary on the New Testament (Grand Rapids: Baker Books, 1998), 31–32.

a fulfillment of the saving promises of the OT to bring about "the obedience of faith for the sake of [Jesus'] name among the all the nations" (1:5).

It was OT Israel who was to serve as a light to the nations and who would inherit the promises made to Abraham through a coming Davidic king (Isa 49). Nevertheless, Paul understands these promises to be fulfilled in the gospel, which centers on Jesus, the "Christ" (1:1), the "seed of David" (1:3), the "Son of God" (1:4), the "Lord" (1:4). Paul views Jesus as the true Israel in whom "God's saving promises for Israel and the Gentiles become a reality."[3]

As this chapter will show, Paul teaches that, as the Son of God, Jesus is the true Israel who fulfills the OT promises, and that those who are united to him through faith constitute the new Israel. This becomes clear by (1) examining the Jewish background for the title "son of God"; (2) observing how Paul appropriates this title for Jesus; and (3) clarifying the relationship between the Church's union with Jesus and its identification as the "sons of God."

THE JEWISH BACKGROUND OF THE "SON OF GOD"

The book of Romans' salutation is among the most theologically complex of the NT Letters. This complexity is highlighted by Paul's claim that the gospel he preaches is in fulfillment of the OT promises of God (1:2). However, at the heart of the good news is Jesus Christ, whom Paul identifies as the "Son of God" (1:3, 4). Most scholars agree that the primary background

---

3. Ibid., 28.

for the title "son of God" is of Jewish origin.[4] Therefore, it is profitable to examine this background with an eye toward understanding its theological significance when applied to Jesus.

Old Testament Context

ADAM

The concept of sonship is first introduced in the creation narrative, specifically as it relates to Adam. Although the title "son of God" is not explicitly used in Genesis 1–3, a connection is made with Adam being created in the "likeness" of God (Gen 1:26).[5] This language of being created in the "image" and "likeness" of God is repeated in Genesis 5:1–3 in reference to Adam fathering Seth. Dempster captures this idea well:

> By juxtaposing the divine creation of Adam in the image of God and the subsequent human creation of Seth in the image of Adam, the transmission of the image of God through this genealogical line is implied, as well as a link between sonship and the image of God. As Seth is a son of Adam, so Adam is a son of God.[6]

---

4. L. W. Hurtado, "Son of God," in *Dictionary of Paul and His Letters* (Downers Grove, IL: InterVarsity Press, 1993), 900. See also G. K. Beale, *A New Testament Biblical Theology: The Unfolding of the Old Testament in the New* (Grand Rapids: Baker Academic, 2011), 401; Thomas R. Schreiner, *New Testament Theology: Magnifying God in Christ* (Grand Rapids: Baker Academic, 2008), 234. Others have argued its origin lies in Greek mystery religions or Gnosticism; Hengel rightly concludes, "This [title] presupposes neither the gnostic myth, which is completely oriented towards protology, nor the timeless myth of Greek and oriental nature religion, but Jewish apocalyptic thought (Martin Hengel, *The Son of God: The Origin of Christology and the History of Jewish Hellenistic Religion* [Eugene, OR: Wipf & Stock Pub, 2007], 35).

5. Beale, *New Testament Biblical Theology*, 401.

6. Stephen G. Dempster, *Dominion and Dynasty: A Biblical Theology of the Hebrew Bible*, New Studies in Biblical Theology 15 (Downers Grove, IL: Inter Varsity Press,

Since Adam is a son of God, understanding his role in the garden is essential to grasping the biblical idea of sonship. Specifically, God gave Adam the unique role as his royal representative, whereby he was to exercise dominion over creation.[7] The first humans were then commissioned by God, who "blessed them. And God said to them, 'Be fruitful and multiply and fill the earth and subdue it, and have dominion over the fish of the sea and over the birds of the heavens and over every living thing that moves on the earth' " (Gen 1:28).

Not only was Adam to exercise rule and dominion in a kingly role, but Genesis 2:4–25 also presents him as a priest serving in the Edenic temple of God.[8] Therefore, as God's king-priest in the garden, Adam was to fulfill the creation mandate given to him in Genesis 1:28 and expand the territory of the garden, so that God's presence would fill the Earth. Instead, Adam allowed the serpent to question God's word, whereby Eve was deceived, and they both partook of the forbidden fruit (3:1–7). From this point forward, the story looks ahead to how God would restore humanity.

ISRAEL

As God's plan for the restoration of humanity and the creation takes shape, the story focuses upon the offspring of

---

2003), 58.

7. Dempster states, "The language used to describe the royal status of the human pair is unambiguous. They are to have dominion (*rādâ*) over the earth and subdue (*kābaš*) it. These words are associated with power and authority" (Dempster, *Dominion and Dynasty*, 59). See also Gentry and Wellum, *Kingdom Through Covenant*, 196.

8. Evidence that Adam assumes a priestly role in the garden is found in Genesis 2:15, where the words "work" (עָבַד) and "keep" (שָׁמַר) appear together. Elsewhere in the OT this pair is used of the priests who keep guard over the ministry of the tabernacle (Num 3:7–8). For a fuller discussion, see G. K. Beale, *The Temple and the Church's Mission: A Biblical Theology of the Dwelling Place of God*, vol. 17, New Studies in Biblical Theology (Downers Grove, IL: InterVarsity Press, 2004), 66–70.

Abraham—Israel. Like Adam, Israel is a son of God. This identification appears in the Exodus narrative, where the nation of
Israel is called God's "firstborn son" (Exod 4:22–23). The idea
of Israel's sonship is found throughout the OT (Isa 1:2; 63:16;
Jer 1:9; Hos 2:23; 11:1) and speaks to "a unique privilege of Israel
as the people chosen and created by Yahweh for himself."[9]
As Beale notes, "The likely reason that Israel was referred
to as God's 'son' or 'firstborn' is that the mantle of Adam has
been passed on to Noah and then to the patriarchs and their
'seed,' Israel."[10] Israel then is presented as a corporate Adam.
This close relationship between Adam and Israel explains
allusions to Genesis 1:28 in the opening of the book of Exodus,
such as, "But the people of Israel were *fruitful* and increased
greatly; they *multiplied* and grew exceedingly strong, so that
the land was filled with them" (Exod 1:7, emphasis mine).

Though Israel was likened to Adam, Israel's task was
slightly different. For instance, unlike Adam who was to exercise dominion over nature and the beasts of the field, Israel
was charged to take possession of the land of Canaan, thus
ruling over the enemies of God. Secondly, after the fall, the
command to be fruitful and multiply became a promise of
what God would do for Abraham's offspring. Nevertheless,
these differences do not overshadow the strong association
between Adam and Israel. Therefore, like Adam, Israel was
to be a kingdom of priests (Exod 19:6). Israel was to exercise

---

9. Brendan Byrne, *Sons of God, Seed of Abraham: A Study of the Idea of the Sonship
of God of All Christians in Paul against the Jewish Background*, Analecta Biblica 83
(Rome: Biblical Institute, 1979), 16.

10. Beale, *New Testament Biblical Theology*, 402. For an overview of the creation
mandate being passed down to Noah, to the patriarchs, and then to Israel, see
N. T. Wright, *The Climax of the Covenant: Christ and the Law in Pauline Theology*
(Minneapolis: Fortress Press, 1992), 21–22.

rule and dominion over the promised land, which was like a new Eden (Exod 3:8, 15:17; cf. Gen 13:10; Psa 78:54; Isa 51:3; Ezek 36:35; Joel 2:3). As God's firstborn son, Israel was to declare the ways of the Lord to the nations and bring them into relationship with him.[11] As Gentry and Wellum note, "In this position [Israel] shows the nations how to have a right relationship to God, how to treat each other in a human way, and how to be faithful stewards of the earth's resources."[12] In other words, Israel was to be God's true humanity, whereby "her land is God's land. Her enemies are God's enemies, and they will be subject to her in the same way that the beasts were subject to Adam."[13] In this way, the nation was to be God's instrument to undo the sin of Adam.

THE DAVIDIC KING

With Israel carrying the mantle of Adam, the descriptions of Israel's king in Adamic language are illuminated: Not only does the nation of Israel bear the title of "son," but so does the Davidic king (2 Sam 7:14; Isa 9:6; Psa 2:7). Following the canonical development of divine sonship, we see that just as Israel assumed the role of Adam, the Davidic king does as well. For example, Deuteronomy 17:14–20 anticipates that Israel would be led by a king who embodies the law of God as the representative for the people.[14] This expectation for the king is the point of 2 Samuel 7:8–17, where God establishes his covenant with David: "I will be to him a father, and he shall be to me a son" (2 Sam 7:14). As God's son, the king stands as the covenant head over God's people, Israel (2 Sam 7:8). Within the

---

11. Gentry and Wellum, *Kingdom Through Covenant*, 398.
12. Ibid., 399.
13. Wright, *The Climax of the Covenant*, 23.
14. Gentry and Wellum, *Kingdom Through Covenant*, 399.

same context, God speaks of his covenant loyalty (חֶסֶד) that will not depart from his son (2 Sam 7:15). This again highlights a special covenantal relationship between God and his son. In light of this privileged relationship with God, one sees that David's status as a son connotes the idea of having dominion and protection.[15] Tangibly, these privileges of sonship include: (1) the Davidic king being exalted (2 Sam 7:9); (2) Israel being given a secured land to dwell in (2 Sam 7:10); (3) Israel given rest from all her enemies (2 Sam 7:11); and (4) a son of David who will sit on the throne forever (2 Sam 7:12–13). Along these lines, the Prophet Isaiah anticipates a day where one will sit on David's throne and will rule justly, and he too is called a "son" (Isa 9:6).

However, as God's son, the Davidic king will not only exercise authority over Israel, but also the nations (Pss 2:7–12; 89:27):

> As the divine son, the Davidic king was to effect the divine instruction or torah in the nation as a whole and was, as a result, a mediator of the Mosaic Torah. However, since the god whom the Davidic king represented was not limited to a local region or territory, but was the creator God and Sovereign of the whole world, the rule of the Davidic king would have repercussions for all the nations, not just for Israel.[16]

This global rule is what God originally intended for Adam in the garden; due to his failure, it was passed down to Israel,

---

15. Byrne, *Sons of God, Seed of Abraham*, 18.
16. Gentry and Wellum, *Kingdom Through Covenant*, 400.

who would be led by a faithful king to restore humanity and the creation.

The expectations that humanity and the creation would be restored through Israel and its faithful king come together in Daniel's apocalyptic vision of the Son of Man (Dan 7). Daniel's vision resounds with echoes of Adam, Israel and Messiah (Dan 7:13). The vision begins with four terrifying beasts who in succession arise out of the sea and are given increasing power to rule over the earth (Dan 7:1–8). However, this destructive reign is brought to an end when the "Ancient of Days" takes his seat on the throne and judges the beasts (Dan 7:9–12). It is at this time that "one like a son of man" (Dan 7:13) comes with the clouds to the Ancient of Days to receive an everlasting kingdom whereby he will reign over all peoples (Dan 7:14).

In Daniel's interpretation of this vision, the four beasts are seen as representatives of four successive kingdoms (Dan 7:17, 23). However, when Daniel interprets the everlasting kingdom given to the "son of man," he speaks of "the saints of the Most High [who] shall receive the kingdom" (Dan 7:18) and rule over all the kingdoms of the earth (Dan 7:27). Daniel's interpretation then identifies this Son of Man with end-time Israel. In other words, like the Davidic king, the Son of Man sums up the people of Israel in himself as its corporate head.

This explanation of the Son of Man's relationship to Israel is confirmed by the identification of the four beasts: In verse 17 the four beasts are referred to as kings, and then later in verse 23 the fourth beast is also called a kingdom. Especially in light of the echoes of Adam, Israel, and the Messiah, this corporate representation of the four beasts is significant. For starters, Daniel's Son of Man represents true humanity, in contrast to the beastly kingdoms of this world. As God's true Adam, this figure then exercises dominion over the beasts like Adam was instructed to do in the garden. Furthermore, the Son of Man is a messianic figure who represents God's people—namely, the saints of Israel, who receive everlasting kingdom (Dan 7:27). With such close thematic parallels between the titles "son of man" and "son of God," it is no wonder that the two are often viewed synonymously within later Jewish literature (e.g., 4QAramaic Apocalypse; *4 Ezra* 13:32, 37, 52).[17]

Summary

Considering the OT background to the title "son of God" and its close association with Daniel's eschatological Son of Man, the status of sonship clearly describes Israel's unique relationship with God. Bearing this title, Israel—as God's true humanity—was to carry out a creation mandate like Adam, exercising dominion over the land and functioning as God's king-priests, mediating God's blessing to the nations. This title was also given to the Davidic king who would represent Israel as a whole. He received the same promises that were given to Israel and, as the covenantal head, served to bring God's promises to fruition. In other words, "Israel will rule the world for God through its appointed king, who will be the son of David."[18] From the OT background alone, the title "son of God" carries the idea of having a privileged relationship with God, whereby those bearing the status of "son" are to exercise dominion over the earth (Dan 7:27) and be God's representative king-priests (Exod 19:5-6). This title then serves as a designation for the people of God, who are the rightful recipients

---

17. For an exhaustive treatment on the relationship between these two titles, see Seyoon Kim, *"The 'Son of Man'" as the Son of God* (Grand Rapids: Eerdmans, 1985).

18. Schreiner, *New Testament Theology*, 235.

of God's kingdom promises. Therefore, the importance of sonship in defining the people of God cannot be overlooked.

Intertestamental Context

After this brief examination of the importance of sonship in the OT, the continued emphasis placed on sonship in later Jewish literature is not surprising. Within Second Temple Judaism, the title "son of God" was also used as a reference to the nation of Israel—an assertion confirmed by several texts that present Israel as God's sons/children and as distinct from the other nations (*Pss. Sol.* 17:30; 18:4–5; *Jub.* 1:25–28, 2:20; Jdt 9:14; Tob 13:4–6; *As. Mos.* 10:3; 3 Macc 5:7–8; 6:3, 28; 7:6–7). In this regard, Byrne concludes that the title "son(s) of God" is essentially "a synonym for the 'People of God', for 'Israel'."[19] Furthermore, like in Daniel 7, the theme of sonship takes on an eschatological nuance anticipating a purified Israel who, as God's true humanity, conquers the surrounding nations. This theme is clearly articulated in *Psalms of Solomon*:

> For [Israel's king] shall know them, that they are all sons of their God. And he shall divide them according to their tribes upon the land, and neither sojourner nor alien shall sojourn with them anymore. He shall judge peoples and nations in the wisdom of his righteousness. Selah. And he shall have the heathen nations to serve him under his yoke; and he shall glorify the Lord in a place to be seen of all the earth; and he

---

19. Byrne, *Sons of God, Seed of Abraham*, 62.

shall purge Jerusalem, making it holy as of old
(*Pss. Sol.* 17:30-33; cf. *Jub.* 1:25ff; *T. Levi* 18:13-14).[20]

During this period, the term "son of God" was also applied
to the Davidic king.[21] For instance, 4QFlor applies 2 Samuel
7:11-14 to the "Shoot of David," and 4QAramaic Apocalypse
(4Q246) refers to a future ruler who will be called "Son of
God ... the son of the most high."[22] Perhaps *4 Ezra* is most clear:
"For my Son the Messiah shall be revealed, together with
those who are with him, and shall rejoice the survivors four
hundred years. And it shall be, after these years that my Son
the Messiah shall die and all in whom there is human breath"
(7:28-29; cf. 13:32, 37, 52; 14:9).[23] Nevertheless, consistent
with the OT (cf. Isa 49; Daniel 7:13-14, 27), a clear delineation
between the nation as a whole and its messianic king is not
readily apparent.

Therefore, in light of such intertestamental literature, the
biblical pattern continues, applying the title "son of God" to
both Israel and the messianic king—thus harkening Israel's
Adam-theology. This title is then reserved exclusively for the
people of God, namely Israel, whereby the coming Davidic
king will lead them to exercise judgment upon the nations
and restore Zion in holiness and purity. Wright provides some
helpful words on this relationship between Adam and Israel
in Jewish literature:

---

20. Charles R. Henry, ed., *Pseudepigrapha of the Old Testament*, vol. 2. (Bellingham, WA: Logos Bible Software, 2004), 649-50.

21. Hengel, *The Son of God*, 42.

22. Directed to these references by Hurtado, "Dictionary of Paul," 901.

23. Henry, *Pseudepigrapha*, 582.

These writings make one large and important point: God's purposes for the human race
in general have devolved onto, and will be fulfilled in, Israel in particular. Israel is, or will become, God's true humanity. What God intended
for Adam will be given to the seed of Abraham.
They will inherit the second Eden, the restored
primeval glory. If there is a "last Adam" in the
relevant Jewish literature, he is not an individual, whether messianic or otherwise. He is the
whole eschatological people of God. If we take
"Adam" language out of this context we do not
merely distort it; we empty it of its basic con-
tent. And if we are to use this material at all for
understanding Paul – as I believe we must – we
cannot ignore its emphases, or imagine that
Paul ignored them, but must ask what he did
with them.[24]

Consequently, when approaching the NT—specifically Paul—
the interconnectivity between sonship, the Christ, and the
people of God is hardly surprising.

Jesus as the "Son of God"

With the Jewish origins of the title "son of God" in mind, we are
now ready to examine Paul's usage of the term in Romans. The
title "Son of God" is first introduced in Romans 1:3, where Paul
says the gospel of God is "concerning his Son."[25] Again, in 1:4,

---

24. Wright, *The Climax of the Covenant*, 20–21.

25. On the one hand, Moo is correct to point out that the participial clause of 1:3
"focuses on the Son of God coming into human existence. This clause assumes the

Paul attributes this status to Jesus, calling him "the Son of God." He uses this designation five other times in Romans (1:9; 5:10; 8:3, 29, 32) highlighting its importance to the argument of the letter. As previously mentioned, Paul wishes to communicate to the Romans that the good news he preaches is in fulfillment of the promises of God in the OT and is centered on God's Son, Jesus Christ our Lord (1:3–4). Although on a popular level, "Son of God" is often understood to be a title referring to Jesus' divinity, it primarily communicates "Jesus' unique status and intimate relationship with God."[26] Therefore, by identifying Jesus as God's Son, Paul imports the Jewish understanding of this title to present Jesus as the true Israel and Davidic king, who will accomplish the creation mandate originally given to Adam.

Jesus as the True Israel

That Paul viewed Jesus as the true Israel is apparent by his identification of Jesus as God's Son. In light of the OT background of this title, it should not surprise us that Paul would identify Jesus with Adam (Rom 5:12–21). Paul even calls Adam a type pointing to Jesus (5:14).[27] The typological relationship

---

preexistence of the Son" (Douglas J. Moo, *The Epistle to the Romans*, New International Commentary on the New Testament [Grand Rapids: Eerdmans, 1996], 46). On the other hand, Schreiner is also apt to observe that "the term 'Son' works at more than one level; it designates Jesus as the true Israel and as the Son who existed before his incarnation" (Schreiner, *Romans*, 38.).

26. Hurtado, "Dictionary of Paul," 900. See also C. E. B. Cranfield, *A Critical and Exegetical Commentary on the Epistle to the Romans*, vol. 1, International Critical Commentary on the Holy Scriptures of the Old and New Testaments (London: T&T Clark International, 2004), 58; Moo, *Romans*, 44.

27. It is beyond the scope of book to iron out the various definitions of typology. However, for the sake of clarity, I have adopted the following definition of "typology" by Greg Beale for this book: "the study of analogical correspondence among revealed truths about persons, events, institutions, and other things within the

between Adam and Christ is monumental, because both of these men stand as representative heads of humanity.[28] I will develop this point further when discussing the Church's union with Christ, but for now, note well that Jesus, as the last Adam, brings "righteousness" (5:16, 18) and "life" (5:17, 21). Jesus is God's obedient Son, who breaks the curse of sin by doing what the first Adam should have done by obeying the Father (5:19).[29]

It should also be noted that as the eschatological Adam, Jesus represents corporate Israel, who also bore the title "son of God" (Exod 4:22–23; Jer 31:9; Hos 11:1; Wis 18:13; *Pss. Sol.* 17:30; 18:4–5; *Jub.* 1:25–28; 2:20; Jdt 9:14; Tob 13:4–6; *As. Mos.* 10:3; 3 Macc 5:7–8; 6:3, 28; 7:6–7). This is consistent with what Paul says elsewhere: that Jesus is the singular seed of Abraham (Gal 3:16) through whom the world is blessed. This is precisely Paul's point. The gospel he preaches is about Jesus, the true Israel, who has fulfilled the promises to Abraham (Rom 4:9–12) to restore creation.

The nation of Israel was to be a kingdom of priests who would serve in order to make known the law of God to the nations and bring them into a right relationship with him. To administer the fulfillment of the Abrahamic covenant, Israel was given the Mosaic law, whereby, through faith, they would experience the blessings of the promises to Abraham

---

historical framework of God's special revelation, which, from a retrospective view, are of a prophetic nature and are escalated in their meaning" (G. K. Beale, *Handbook on the New Testament Use of the Old Testament: Exegesis and Interpretation* [Grand Rapids: Baker Academic, 2012], 14).

28. Thomas R. Schreiner, *Paul, Apostle of God's Glory in Christ: A Pauline Theology* (Downers Grove, IL: InterVarsity Press, 2006), 158. See also Constantine R. Campbell, who rightly distinguishes "representation" from "corporate personality" (Constantine R. Campbell, *Paul and Union with Christ: An Exegetical and Theological Study* [Grand Rapids: Zondervan, 2012], 343–47).

29. Beale, *New Testament Biblical Theology*, 428.

and extend these blessings to the nations.[30] Furthermore, the law of Moses was given to "show them how to be [God's] true humanity. It will direct, guide, and lead them to have a right relationship with God and a right relationship with everyone else in the covenant community. It will also teach them how to have a right relationship to all the creation."[31] In other words, Israel was a corporate Adam who was to exercise dominion over the creation until the knowledge of God filled the earth. Nevertheless, Israel failed to be obedient, because like the other nations, it too was in Adam.

Therefore, it is imperative to see that "Jesus' two roles as the last Adam and true Israel are two sides of one redemptive-historical coin."[32] As the Son of God, Jesus succeeds where both Adam and Israel (a corporate Adam) failed, by extending the knowledge of God to all peoples through faith in him. Specifically, Paul argues that Jesus brought about the fulfillment of the law (Rom 3:27–31) and extended God's saving promises to the nations (Rom 1:5, 13; 3:29; 4:17–24; 9:24, 30; 11:11, 12, 13, 25; 15:9–12, 16, 18, 27; 16:26).

Jesus as Davidic King

Returning to Paul's opening statements in Romans, he not only identifies Jesus as God's Son, but as God's "Son, who was descended from David according to the flesh and was appointed to be the Son of God in power according to the Spirit of holiness by his resurrection from the dead" (Rom 1:3–4). The relationship between what Paul has asserted in 1:2 and

---

30. Gentry and Wellum, *Kingdom Through Covenant*, 304.

31. Ibid.

32. Beale, *New Testament Biblical Theology*, 428.

what he says about Jesus' Davidic status cannot be ignored. Jesus as the Son of David fulfills what the OT prophets foretold concerning a righteous king to rule over Israel and the nations (2 Sam 7:12–16; Isa 11:1–5, 10; Jer 23:5–6; 33:14–17; Ezek 34:23–24; 37:24–25).

Here, we must attend to the exact meaning of τοῦ ὁρισθέντος in verse 4 so that the significance of Jesus' "appointment to be the Son of God" is not overlooked. Many modern translations render this participial clause "who was declared to be the Son of God" (e.g., ESV, NASB, HCSB). Understood this way, Jesus, who is eternally God's Son, is shown to be the Son of God by the power of the resurrection. Although theologically true, this is not Paul's point. The verb does not mean "to declare" or "to show." Throughout the NT, it always carries the meaning, "fix," "determine," or "appoint" (Luke 22:22; Acts 2:23; 10:42; 11:29; 17:26, 31; Heb 4:7).[33] Despite what may appear as a theological difficulty, one should translate τοῦ ὁρισθέντος in Romans 1:4 as "who was appointed." Here, Paul is likely alluding to Psalm 2:7, where the son of David is "decreed" to be the anointed king over the nations.[34] Schreiner captures this idea well:

> The idea here, then, is not that Jesus was "declared" or "shown to be" at the resurrection what he was all along, namely, the eternal Son of God. Rather, the point is that Jesus was "appointed" to be God's Son in power at the resurrection of the dead. He was exalted to a level of power and authority that he did not have previously.[35]

33. Cranfield, *Romans*, 1:61.
34. Robert Jewett, *Romans: A Commentary*, Hermeneia (Minneapolis: Fortress Press, 2007), 104; Schreiner, *Romans*, 41–42.
35. Schreiner, *Romans*, 41–42.

Jesus, by virtue of his resurrection from the dead, is appointed as the Davidic king, who is the Son of God.

There may also be a further allusion to Psalm 2 in Paul's
reference to his apostolic mission "to bring about the obedience of faith for the sake of his name among all the nations"
(1:5). If so, Paul sees his apostolic mission to be a fulfillment
of God's promise to give the nations as an inheritance to his
Son (Psa 2:8).[36] This connection between Psalm 2 and Paul's
apostolic mission is consistent with what Paul says in Romans
15:8–13, where he summarizes the themes of the entire letter.[37]
In these verses Paul quotes from Psalms (15:9, 11), the Torah
(15:10), and the Prophets (15:12) to show that through the ministry (διάκονος, 15:8) of Christ, the Davidic king, the promises of
Abraham have been fulfilled whereby both Jews and Gentiles
are united together in worshiping and praising God.[38] In verse
9, Paul first cites Psalm 18:49.[39] The context of this psalm is
David's victory in being delivered from all his enemies and
from the hand of Saul (cf. 2 Sam 22:1). The praise David offers
in this psalm shows that he is the rightful king who has been
exalted (2 Sam 22:48). As the king, not only were these victo-
ries David's, but as verse 50 suggests, they were also shared
by "his offspring" (cf. 2 Sam 22:51). This idea of a shared victory is substantial: David is the speaker in whom the nation
of Israel is corporately represented singing praises to God
for giving him victory over the Gentiles.[40] I suggest that Paul

---

36. Hurtado, "Dictionary of Paul," 904.
37. Schreiner, *Romans*, 752.
38. Moo, *Romans*, 878.
39. The citation also could be from 2 Samuel 22:50. Moo says, "The LXX text
of these two verses is identical, except for the placement of the vocative κύριε,
which Paul omits. With this exception, Paul's text reproduces the LXX exactly"
(ibid., 878n36).
40. Schreiner, *Romans*, 757.

uses this text typologically to show its fulfillment in the new David, Jesus. So, in the same way, Jesus represents Israel, and because of his victory the Gentiles are included with the Jews in praising God.

Paul again presents Jesus as the promised Davidic king in Romans 15:12 by citing Isaiah 11:10 (LXX): "the root of Jesse will come, even he who arises to rule the Gentiles; in him will the Gentiles hope." The Prophet Isaiah speaks of a day of restoration that will occur after severe judgment has come upon Israel. The entire line of David will have been removed, but nevertheless a "shoot shall come forth from the stump of Jesse and a branch from his roots shall bear fruit" (Isa 11:1). Essentially Isaiah is looking forward to a day when "the Lord will begin afresh and create a new David out of the 'stump of Jesse.' "[41] This new Davidic king will judge with righteousness (Isa 11:3-5), he will bring about the restoration of the earth (Isa 11:6-9), he will restore the remnant of Israel from the nations (Isa 11:11-16), and of him the nations will inquire (Isa 11:10). Paul's identification of Jesus as Isaiah's new David is then critical to the claim that Jesus is the true Israel. However, before continuing with Paul's argument in Romans 15, we must engage further with how the Prophet Isaiah links the eschatological David with the Servant of the Lord.

In Isaiah, this Servant will be given as a covenant for God's people, to be a light for the nations and bring deliverance to those in captivity (Isa 49:6). The Lord's Servant is identified as Israel (Isa 49:3), who will bring about the restoration of the nation (Isa 49:5). Although it is difficult to discern whether

---

41. Mark A. Seifrid, "Romans," in *Commentary on the New Testament Use of the Old Testament* (Grand Rapids: Baker Academic, 2007), 686.

the Servant should be identified with the nation of Israel or with an individual, it is best to view the Servant as the future Davidic king who will rule as Israel's covenant head.[42] In Isaiah 37:35, the Lord refers to the future Davidic king as his servant. Furthermore, as has already been shown, the Davidic king represented the nation of Israel. This corporate representation is exactly what is seen in Isaiah 49 and is how Israel's commission of blessing the nations would be fulfilled. Therefore, the Servant functions as a representative of Israel.[43]

Returning to Romans 15:12, Paul quotes Isaiah 11:10 (LXX) in order to present Jesus as Isaiah's new David who has come to rule over the Gentiles. However, this rule is not one of judgment, but rather of salvation. This salvation is precisely what the Lord commissions his Servant to accomplish in Isaiah 49:6 when he says, "It is too light a thing that you should be my servant to raise up the tribes of Jacob and to bring back the preserved of Israel; I will make you as a light for the nations, that my salvation may reach to the end of the earth."

---

42. With a casual reading of this verse one might conclude the Servant is not an individual, but rather the nation Israel. This interpretation is somewhat understandable since the nation Israel is said to be Yahweh's servant elsewhere in Isaiah (Isa 41:8, 9; 42:19; 43:10; 44:1, 2, 21, 26; 45:4; 48:20). Nevertheless, there are several reasons for viewing the Servant in Isaiah 49 as an individual. First, the Servant is a human being who was born of a woman (Isa 49:1b). Second, this Servant is said to bring restoration to Israel (49:5). Third, assuming that Isaiah 49:1–7 is a development of 42:1–7, this Servant is given as a covenant for Israel (42:6; 49:8); a light for the nations (42:6; 49:6); to open the eyes of the blind (42:7); and to bring deliverance from bondage (42:7; 49:9). In contrast to the Servant, Israel had broken God's covenant (1:2ff); had despised God's name among the nations (52:5); is blind and deaf (35:5); and has been sold into exile (5:13). For an excellent treatment of the identity of the Servant in Isaiah 40–55, see Mark Gignilliat, "Who Is Isaiah's Servant? Narrative Identity and Theological Potentiality," *Scottish Journal of Theology* 61, no. 2 (2008): 125–36.

43. John N. Oswalt, *The Book of Isaiah: Chapters 40–66* (Grand Rapids: Eerdmans, 1998), 291.

In Romans, Paul understands this salvation, which has come not only for the Jews but also the Gentiles, as accomplished by Jesus' sacrificial death (Rom 4:23–25; 8:32). Paul says that it is Jesus "who was delivered up (παρεδόθη) for our trespasses" (4:25). This phrase recalls Isaiah 53, where the Servant of the Lord suffers on behalf of the sins of Israel (Isa 53:5, 10, 11, 12). Again, Paul alludes to Isaiah 53 when he says that the Father "did not spare his own Son but gave him up for us all" (Rom 8:32).[44] Note that the Prophet Isaiah identifies this Servant to be the true Israel (Isa 49:3), who, by his sufferings, fulfills the promises of deliverance from exile (Isa 40–66).[45] Therefore, by equating Jesus with Isaiah's Suffering Servant, Paul also sees Jesus as the true Israel.

Such conclusions pose serious challenges for dispensationalists like Robert Saucy, who contends that Isaiah only pictures "Israel as a corporate personality in which the head first ministers to the body in order that the body may then accomplish its mission through the head."[46] In other words, dispensationalists merely see the Messiah as the representative of Israel to restore the nation to accomplish its original mission. Saucy continues to say, "That this use of 'Israel' for Christ as the head of the corporate people of Israel does not include Gentiles is seen in the fact that Christ never applied

---

44. Moo rightly notes that Paul's use of παραδίδωμι is taken from Isaiah 53. He says, "The verb, παραδίδωμι, which is prominent especially in the Gospel passion predictions, and is picked up from LXX Isa. 53, where it is used three times to describe the 'handing over' of the suffering Servant. ... Paul also uses the word frequently with reference to Jesus' death – sometimes as here, of the Father's 'handing him over to death' " (Moo, *Romans*, 540n19). See also Cranfield, *Romans*, 1:436; Schreiner, *Romans*, 459–60.

45. Schreiner, *Romans*, 243.

46. Robert L Saucy, *The Case for Progressive Dispensationalism: The Interface Between Dispensational & Non-Dispensational Theology* (Grand Rapids: Zondervan, 1993), 191.

this name to himself, nor did the early church ever call Jesus 'Israel.' "[47]

The difficulty with Saucy's position is that it goes precisely against Paul's interpretation of Isaiah: Paul understands Jesus to be the true Israel promised in Isaiah who, by his sacrificial death, brought about salvation for both Jews and Gentiles (1:16; 10:9–13). In other words, Jesus is the Servant of the Lord whom God handed over "for us all" (ὑπὲρ ἡμῶν πάντων, 8:32), not just the nation Israel. Paul purposely uses inclusive language to show that the Gentiles are included along with the Jews in benefiting from the Suffering Servant's sacrifice.[48] So Paul does not see Jesus as merely restoring the nation of Israel so it can bless the nations; instead, Jesus as the true Israel accomplishes this task in himself. He brings about the fulfillment of Isaiah's new creation promises of deliverance from exile, the new covenant blessings and Abrahamic covenant blessings in the Church.[49] More will be said about the inauguration of the new creation in the following chapter, but for now, suffice it to say that a future restoration of Israel to accomplish these things would be unnecessary.

In summary, it is important to understand that Paul presents Jesus as the Davidic king, the true Son of God, who embodies his people Israel to fulfill God's promise of blessing the nations and making God's presence known in all the

---

47. Ibid., 191.

48. James D. G. Dunn, *Romans 1–8*, Word Biblical Commentary 38a (Nashville: Thomas Nelson, 1988), 501.

49. Contra, Michael G. Vanlaningham, "The Jewish People According to the Book of Romans," in *The People, the Land, and the Future of Israel: Israel and the Jewish People in the Plan of God* (Grand Rapids: Kregel Publications, 2014), 128–29; Michael J. Vlach, "What Does Christ as 'True Israel' Mean for the Nation Israel?: A Critique of the Non-Dispensational Understanding," *The Master's Seminary Journal* 23, no. 1 (2012): 44.

earth. What is noteworthy is that if Jesus is God's true Son and Davidic king who embodies Israel, then God's people are now defined by being rightly related to him. This reality therefore explains how the Gentiles are able to become heirs of these promises, which at one time seemed only available for the nation Israel.

THE CHURCH'S UNION WITH JESUS

Paul's appropriation of sonship to Christ primarily identifies him as the true Israel and the promised Davidic king. Functioning as the covenant head over God's people, it is through Christ that "God's purposes for creation are realized, including his purposes for Israel."[50] Therefore, it is not surprising that in Romans Paul applies the same status of sonship to all those who are united to Christ by faith (8:14–17). Paul understands that

> In Christ, the antitype of Israel, all of God's promises are yes and amen. We, as the church, the people of Christ receive all the benefits of his glorious, effective, and triumphant word *by virtue of our faith union with him.* He, as our covenant head, wins for us our redemption, and all that he has achieved becomes ours due to that union.[51]

It is through union with Christ that Gentiles are grafted into the people of God (11:17) and inherit the privileged blessings of Israel (8:15). However, Vlach rejects this idea, instead

---

50. Gentry and Wellum, *Kingdom Through Covenant*, 690.
51. Ibid.

suggesting that union with Christ does not provide this status and does not present the Church as the new Israel.[52] Vlach further argues that Scripture does present Jesus as the "ideal" or "true Israel," but that Christ does not replace the nation's mediator role to be a light to the Gentiles.[53] The difficulty with Vlach's position is that it conflicts with Paul's words in 15:8–13, where Christ serves to extend the promises of God to the Gentiles (15:8–9), thus fulfilling what the nation of Israel failed to do. This inclusion of the Gentiles is made possible through union with Christ as the mediator of the promises of God. According to this reading of Romans 15:8–13, dispensationalists are holding out for a future role of ethnic Israel that is already being carried out by Jesus, through his Church.

Expressions of Union in Romans

In Romans Paul expresses the believer's union with Christ in various ways.[54] The most popular expression is that believers are said to be ἐν Χριστῷ. Under this formula believers are (1) justified through the redemption that is in Christ (ἐν Χριστῷ, 3:24); (2) believers are made alive to God in Christ (ἐν Χριστῷ, 6:11); (3) believers have eternal life by a gift of God in Christ (ἐν Χριστῷ, 6:23); (4) there is no condemnation for those in Christ (ἐν Χριστῷ, 8:1); (5) believers have been set free from the law of sin and death in Christ (ἐν Χριστῷ, 8:2); (6) the love of God is found in Christ (ἐν Χριστῷ, 8:39); and (7) believers are incorporated into one body in Christ (ἐν Χριστῷ, 12:5).[55]

---

52. Vlach, "What Does Christ as 'True Israel' Mean for the Nation Israel?," 44.
53. Ibid., 54.
54. For an exhaustive treatment on the subject of Paul and union with Christ, see Campbell, *Paul and Union with Christ*.
55. Ibid., 67–199.

Paul also uses other expressions to communicate the reality that believers are united with Christ. These include: (1) εἰς Χριστὸν, believers are baptized into Christ (6:3), denoting one's identification with him; (2) σὺν Χριστῷ, believers have died with Christ (6:8), being associated with him in his death; and (3) διὰ Χριστοῦ, believers have peace with God through Christ (5:1) and so they will reign in life (5:17).[56]

Although this discussion is not an exhaustive treatment of union in Romans, it should be evident that union with Christ is a dominant theme, significant to the argument of the letter. The dominance of this theme explains why Paul sees Christ as central to the gospel he preaches: namely, the promises and blessings of God find their fulfillment in him, the true Israel. Therefore, it follows that those who are united to Jesus are the heirs of these blessings. Paul assures believers of these things in Romans 5:12–21. As one examines this text more closely, these promises are secured because of what Christ has accomplished for those whose identity is in him.

Union with the New Adam

When discussing union with Christ it is essential to address Paul's Adam Christology. Having already seen that Jesus bears the title "Son of God" it is fitting that he would also be called the "last Adam" (1 Cor 15:45). In Romans 5:12–21 Paul presents Adam and Christ as the two representative heads over humanity. On the one hand, the first Adam represents the old creation, which is ruled by sin, death, and judgment (15:12, 16, 18). On the other hand, the last Adam represents the new creation where righteousness and life reign (15:16, 17, 18, 21).

---

56. Ibid., 200–40.

Earlier in Romans Paul argued that "there is no distinction" (3:22b) between Jew and Gentile, because "all have sinned and fall short of the glory of God" (3:23). Paul universalizes humanity because all are naturally "in Adam" who, by his disobedience, allowed sin and death to enter the world and so rule over his posterity. However, to be "in Christ" is to share in the new creation marked by righteousness and life.[57] This participation in the new creation is consistent with Paul's other writings where he says those who are "in Christ" are "a new creation" (2 Cor 5:17).

Chapters 5–8 signal a new section in Romans, which is characterized by hope.[58] It is the hope that believers share in God's glory (5:2; 8:18, 30), having been justified (5:1, 9; 6:7; 8:30, 33), having peace with God (5:1; 8:6), and being loved by God (5:5, 8; 8:35, 39), despite the threat of tribulation and suffering.[59] As we'll see in the next chapter of this book, God's promises regarding a future with him can be encapsulated in the new creation, which was for Israel (Isa 65:17–25). In the first four chapters of Romans, Paul has argued that "God's saving promises made in the OT have been fulfilled, that they are available for all peoples, and that they are secured through faith."[60] Now, in Romans 5:12–21, Paul presents Christ as the head over the new creation, wherein all who are united to him by faith share. Therefore, Schreiner is correct to assert, "The church is a new society that expresses in part what God intended when he made Adam and Eve. The saving promises made to Abraham are becoming a reality in Christ since he

---

57. Gentry and Wellum, *Kingdom Through Covenant*, 616–17; Schreiner, *Paul*, 158–59.
58. Moo, *Romans*, 293; Schreiner, *Romans*, 246.
59. Moo, *Romans*, 293.
60. Schreiner, *Romans*, 246.

reverses the curse and devastation imposed on the world through the first Adam."[61]

In sum, this "new society" is the new Israel in Christ. Christ represents those who are united to him, so that what he inherits is also theirs (8:17, 32). Therefore, because of this union with God's Son, believers are also called "sons of God" (8:19) and are being conformed into the image of the Son (8:29). And as children of God, believers eagerly await "the glory that is to be revealed to us" (8:18), namely a new creation (8:21).

Summary

Significant ground has been covered in this chapter, serving as a foundation for the forthcoming chapters. First, we surveyed the Jewish background to the title "son of God." From this overview, we discovered that the title "son of God" was initially applied to Adam but later placed upon the nation of Israel and the Davidic king. As God's son, Israel was to be led by its king and carry the mantle of exercising dominion over an Eden-like land and serving as God's king-priests. Therefore, in light of the OT alone, the title "son of God" carries the idea of having a privileged relationship with God, whereby those bearing the status of "son" are to exercise dominion over God's enemies and be God's representative king-priests. This definition also held true as the intertestamental context for the title "son of God" was examined. Similar to the OT context, the title was used synonymously for the people of God, namely Israel, through whom the coming Messiah and Davidic king would exercise judgment upon the nations and restore Zion.

---

61. Schreiner, *Paul*, 159.

Having examined the Jewish background to the title "son of God," we then saw that Paul imports this understanding when he appropriates the title to Jesus. As a result, Paul not only identifies Jesus as true Israel, but as Israel's Davidic king. Therefore, as God's true Son who embodies Israel, God's people are now defined by rightly being related to him.

Finally, we looked at the Church's union with Christ in Romans and saw that those united to Jesus no longer have Adam as their representative head. Rather, they are "in Christ" and so too bear the title "sons of God," thus identifying them as the new Israel and rightful heirs of the new creation. With this foundation laid, we are now in a position to inspect more closely how the promises to Israel concerning a new creation have been inaugurated in Christ and are mediated to the Church. This reality will then explain how Paul is able to take OT titles and images originally given to Israel and apply them to the Church throughout Romans.

CHAPTER 3

The Inauguration of the New Creation

Paul begins Romans by declaring that his gospel is a fulfillment of the promised deliverance from exile spoken by the prophets (1:1-2; cf. Isa 52:7). Isaiah closely links this so-called new exodus with God's promise of a new creation (Isa 42:9; 43:18-19; 48:6-7; 65:17; 66:22).[1] Woven throughout Romans, Paul affirms that the blessings of the new creation have invaded the present. The good news that he preaches is not limited to Jews, but is for everyone who believes (1:16). Since God's redemption has extended to the Gentiles, the promises to Abraham are being fulfilled (4:16-18). In addition, for those in Christ, the promised Spirit has been poured out, circumcising their hearts, thus enabling them to observe the law (2:25-29; 8:1-4). That all are the rightful recipients of these blessings through faith is consistent with what we saw

---

1. Thomas R. Schreiner, *Paul, Apostle of God's Glory in Christ: A Pauline Theology* (Downers Grove, IL: InterVarsity Press, 2006), 269.

in the previous chapter—that believers are united to Christ and so bear the title "sons of God," thus identifying them as the new Israel and rightful heirs of the new creation.

Next, we'll see that Jesus is the true Israel and those united to him become the new Israel by tracing Paul's new creation motif throughout Romans. In particular, I will argue that God's saving promises to Israel concerning a new creation have been inaugurated in Christ and are experienced in the Church through union with him. That the future new creation has invaded the present is made evident by the fact that Paul sees the new exodus, the new covenant, and the Abrahamic covenant as fulfilled in the Church. If such is the case, it is difficult not to see the Church as the new Israel in Christ.

THE NEW EXODUS

Gospel

In the opening paragraph of Romans, Paul presents his gospel as fulfilling the saving promises of God to Israel (1:1-2). As Wagner states, "[Paul] is convinced that, despite its radical newness, the gospel he preaches stands in deep continuity with the witness of the biblical texts to God's continuing faithfulness to the covenant with Israel."[2] However, it is this "radical newness" of Paul's gospel that he understands as actually fulfilling the OT in a greater way than was expected

---

2. J. Ross Wagner, *Heralds of the Good News: Isaiah and Paul "in Concert" in the Letter to the Romans*, Supplements to Novum Testamentum v. 101 (Boston: Brill, 2002), 11. See also Richard B. Hays, *Echoes of Scripture in the Letters of Paul* (New Haven, CT: Yale University Press, 1989), 157-60.

(Rom 9–11).[3] In particular, Paul pictures the OT promises of a new exodus, where Israel would experience both physical and spiritual restoration, as currently being fulfilled in the Church. The present fulfillment of the new exodus is immediately apparent by Paul's use of the word εὐαγγέλιον ("gospel").[4] The term "gospel" recalls the good news of Israel's deliverance from Babylonian exile (Isa 40:9; 52:7; 60:6; 61:1 LXX) and its future restoration (Isa 42:9; 43:18–19; 48:6–7; 65:17; 66:22 LXX).[5]

For Paul the gospel "is the power of God for salvation to everyone who believes" (Rom 1:16), because "in it the righteousness of God is revealed" (1:17). Most commentators agree that verses 16–17 serve as the theme or thesis for the entire letter.[6] This assumption is correct, for much of Paul's vocabulary in Romans is introduced by mentioning "gospel," "salvation," "faith," or "righteousness."[7] Furthermore, it is the proclamation of the gospel that Paul has been set apart as an apostle (1:1). It is the gospel for which he wishes to preach when he comes to Rome (1:15). And the gospel is what he longs to bring to Spain (15:20–24).

Paul wishes to preach the gospel where Christ is not yet named (15:20) because it has the power to effect salvation. More will be said about this later, but for now, it suffices to say that Paul's references to salvation include the saving promises

3. Thomas R. Schreiner, *Romans*, Baker Exegetical Commentary on the New Testament (Grand Rapids: Baker Books, 1998), 38.

4. Paul uses both the noun εὐαγγέλιον and the verb εὐαγγελίζω throughout Romans (1:1, 9, 15, 16; 2:16; 10:15, 16; 11:28; 15:16, 19, 20; 16:25).

5. N. T. Wright, *The New Testament and the People of God* (Minneapolis: Fortress Press, 1992), 332.

6. C. K. Barrett, *The Epistle to the Romans*, Black's New Testament Commentaries (London: Continuum, 1991), 27; Cranfield, *Romans*, 1:87; Dunn, *Romans 1–8*, 38; Jewett, *Romans*, 135; R. D. Kaylor, *Paul's Covenant Community: Jew and Gentile in Romans* (Atlanta: John Knox Press, 1988), 30; Moo, *Romans*, 64; Schreiner, *Romans*, 59.

7. Kaylor, *Paul's Covenant Community*, 30.

of deliverance made to Israel in the OT.[8] Significantly, however, Paul does not limit the recipients of these promises to the Jews. Rather, Paul says it is for "everyone who believes, for the Jew first and also to the Greek" (1:16). This theme of the universality of the gospel permeates the entire letter (2:5–11; 3:9, 22–23, 29–30; 4:9–12, 16–17; 9:24; 10:11–13; 11:32; 15:8–12). It is not surprising, then, that Paul presents believing Gentiles as fellow recipients of OT promises along with believing Jews through faith in the gospel.

That Paul views his gospel as the fulfillment of Israel's promise of a new exodus is evident in Romans 10:14–21. These verses are part of a larger section (Rom 9–11) where Paul defends his gospel against the charge that the word of God has failed (9:6) because most of ethnic Israel has not believed and so obtained the Abrahamic promises. In 10:8–13, Paul details the connection between "the word of faith" (10:8) that he preaches and the response to that message. Citing Isaiah 28:16 and Joel 2:32, he asserts that the one who "believes" (10:9, 11) and "who calls on the name of the Lord" (10:13) will share in God's salvation and righteousness (10:9, 10, 13). In verses 14–21 Paul retraces the steps by which one will "call" upon the Lord and so be saved. He does this through the use of four rhetorical questions, which culminate with the need for preachers to bring good news. In 10:15, Paul responds to his last question with a citation from Isaiah 52:7[9] "revealing the crucial role that

---

8. Schreiner, *Romans*, 61.

9. Although Paul's citation is closer to the MT over the LXX, he does stray from both in his use of the plural τῶν εὐαγγελιζομένων. Moo says this "manifests his desire to make the text applicable to the multitude of Christian preachers" (Moo, *Romans*, 663n12).

his own mission plays in the outworking of God's redemptive purpose."[10]

Isaiah 52:7 is a part of God's prophecy concerning the deliverance of Israel from Babylonian captivity. Wagner states, "The long-awaited deliverance from exile, promised to God's people at various points throughout Isaiah, at last finds it realization as heralds come bounding over the mountains to Jerusalem with the triumphant cry, 'Your God shall reign!' "[11] It is these messengers—whom Isaiah spoke about in 40:1–9— who were to announce the Lord's return to Zion, whereby he would redeem his people. Paul understands Isaiah's new exodus as finding its fulfillment in the apostolic preaching of Jesus' death, burial, and resurrection. Paul is saying that "messengers have been sent out, the good news is being preached, the return from exile is at hand, and this salvation is now available to both Jews and Gentiles."[12]

Paul's point is that the Jews cannot say they have not heard the good news, for it has gone out into the world, just as the OT said it would (10:18; cf. Psa 19:4). Not only have the Jews heard it, but they actually understood it (10:19–20; cf. Deut 32:21; Isa 65:1, 2). However, Israel has refused to believe the message (10:21; cf. 10:16). Nevertheless, in order to make Israel jealous (10:19), God has extended his offer of eschatological salvation to the Gentiles (10:19–20). This inclusion of the Gentiles is consistent with what we have seen throughout Romans. The people of God are not defined by their ethnicity, but rather through faith in the gospel of God's Son—being

---

10. Wagner, *Heralds of the Good News*, 170.

11. Ibid., 174.

12. Schreiner, *Romans*, 568.

rightly related to the true Israel, whereby one shares in the restoration promises of the OT.

Romans 15:16 provides additional evidence that Paul views his preaching of the gospel as fulfillment of the promises of a new exodus. Here, Paul identifies himself as "a minister (λειτουργὸν) of Christ Jesus to the Gentiles in the priestly service (ἱερουργοῦντα) of the gospel of God, so that the offering of the Gentiles may be acceptable, sanctified by the Holy Spirit." Paul's use of the word λειτουργός could simply refer to him as a "minister" or "servant." However, coupling it with "the sacrificial language in the latter part of the verse makes it more likely that he intends the term to connote *priestly* ministry specifically."[13]

The proclamation of the gospel then is an act of priestly service. In this service, Paul presents the Gentiles as an offering to God.[14] Paul likely views this offering of the Gentiles as fulfilling Isaiah 66:20.[15] Leading up to this verse, Isaiah declares that in the last days the nations will see God's glory (Isa 66:18–19). He then says, "They shall bring all your brothers from all the nations as an offering to the Lord" (Isa 66:20). These "brothers" are the converted Gentiles from the nations who become part of the one people of God.[16] In Romans 15:16,

---

13. Moo, *Romans*, 889.

14. Most commentators agree that in the phrase ἡ προσφορὰ τῶν ἐθνῶν the genitive ἐθνῶν is appositional. Therefore, it is not the Gentiles who bring an offering to God, but rather Paul offers the Gentiles as the offering. See James D. G. Dunn, *Romans 9–16*, Word Biblical Commentary 38b (Nashville: Thomas Nelson, 1988), 860; C. E. B. Cranfield, *A Critical and Exegetical Commentary on the Epistle to the Romans*, vol. 2, International Critical Commentary on the Holy Scriptures of the Old and New Testaments (London: T&T Clark International, 2004), 756n3; Schreiner, *Romans*, 767.

15. Schreiner, *Romans*, 767.

16. Contra Dunn who understands Isaiah 66:20 to speak of "diaspora Jews who form the eschatological offering" (Dunn, *Romans 9–16*, 860.). More likely Isaiah

Paul perceives his gospel ministry as the fulfillment of this eschatological event.

Paul then continues to say that signs and wonders accompany the bringing of the Gentiles to obedience, by the power of the Spirit of God (15:18–19). This language recalls how God brought Israel out of Egypt by the power of signs and wonders (Exod 7:3; Deut 4:34; 6:22; 7:19; 26:8; 34:11; Neh 9:10; Psa 104:27 LXX).[17] Paul expresses that the signs and wonders accomplished through him point to the inauguration of the new exodus and the new age. This is confirmed in 15:21, where Paul cites Isaiah 52:15 in support of preaching the gospel where Christ is yet to be named. This verse from Isaiah is part of the Servant Songs, where the Gentiles who have not seen or understood the message of the Servant of the Lord will be enlightened. Like in Romans 10, Paul sees himself as the herald of this good news of deliverance from exile, which comes from the true Israel, Jesus.

Resurrection

Jesus Christ and his resurrection are therefore central to Paul's gospel (Rom 1:4). The resurrection harkens back to Israel's promises of return from exile (Isa 26:19; Ezek 37:1–4) and signifies the inauguration of the new creation.[18] Paul regularly refers to the resurrection in the book of Romans (1:4; 4:24–25; 6:4–5, 11–13; 7:4; 8:11; 10:9). And as mentioned above,

---

speaks of the eschatological offering of the Gentiles who are incorporated into the one people of God. For a defense of this interpretation, see Peter J. Gentry and Stephen J. Wellum, *Kingdom Through Covenant: A Biblical-Theological Understanding of the Covenants* (Wheaton, IL: Crossway, 2012), 457–60.

17. Schreiner, *Romans*, 768.

18. Ibid., 44–45.

the resurrection of Christ is to be viewed as the fulfillment of the OT promises (10:1–4). J. R. Daniel Kirk goes so far as to suggest that the theme of resurrection is the hermeneutical key to interpreting Paul's purpose in Romans.[19] Although this may be an overstatement, it is true that Paul envisions Christ's resurrection as fundamental to the gospel and the basis for hope in the fulfillment of God's promises.

This importance placed on the resurrection is consistent with understandings of resurrection in the OT and Second Temple Judaism. Wright has persuasively argued that the resurrection of the dead in Judaism is inseparable from the promises of return from exile and the fulfillment of the new creation.[20] He says:

> Thus the Jews who believed in resurrection did so as one part of a larger belief in the renewal of the whole created order. Resurrection would be, in one and the same moment, the reaffirmation of the covenant and the reaffirmation of creation. Israel would be restored within a restored cosmos: the world would see, at last, who had all along been the true people of the creator god.[21]

---

19. J. R. Daniel Kirk, *Unlocking Romans: Resurrection and the Justification of God* (Grand Rapids: Eerdmans, 2008), 55.
20. Wright, *The New Testament and the People of God*, 320–34. See also Kirk, who suggests that the resurrection of the dead in Judaism had four functions: (1) providing vindication for Israel and God; (2) motiving God's people for righteous behavior; (3) securing the restoration of the cosmos; and (4) the restoration of the Israel (Kirk, *Unlocking Romans*, 15).
21. Wright, *The New Testament and the People of God*, 332.

Wright is correct, for in turning to the prophets one sees that the resurrection is linked to the promises of restoration. For example, the Prophet Ezekiel says that God will bring about a spiritual renewal of Israel. This renewal will consist of a "new heart" and a "new spirit" (Ezek 36:26); God says he will "cause you to walk in my statutes and be careful to obey my rules. You shall dwell in the land that I gave to your fathers, and you shall be my people, and I will be your God" (Ezek 36:27–28). In Ezekiel 37 these promises are set in the context of resurrection.[22] In 37:12–14 the prophet writes:

> Therefore prophesy, and say to them, Thus says the Lord GOD: Behold, I will open your graves and raise you from your graves, O my people. And I will bring you into the land of Israel. And you shall know that I am the LORD, when I open your graves, and raise you from your graves, O my people. And I will put my Spirit within you, and you shall live, and I will place you in your own land. Then you shall know that I am the LORD; I have spoken, and I will do it, declares the LORD.

What is seen here is a close connection with Israel's restoration to the land coupled with spiritual and physical resurrection.[23] Isaiah also links the promises of Israel's deliverance with resurrection when he says, "Your dead shall live; their bodies shall rise. You who dwell in the dust, awake and sing

---

22. Beale, *New Testament Biblical Theology*, 252.
23. Ibid.

for joy! For your dew is a dew of light, and the earth will give birth to the dead" (Isa 26:19).

Returning to Romans, Christ's resurrection marks the initial fulfillment of God's promises of resurrection for Israel (Rom 1:1–4). This truth explains why Paul's gospel (εὐαγγέλιον) is considered the good news of God's salvation (1:16). However, this good news made possible by the resurrection of Jesus is not only for the Jews, but for "everyone who believes" (1:16). This inclusion of the Gentiles is made possible because Jesus' resurrection is the basis for the believer's resurrection. Again, it is through union with Christ that one receives the promises of God.

No doubt in Romans 6–8, Paul draws upon much of what was promised in the OT concerning resurrection and deliverance from exile. For instance, in 6:1–4, Paul says believers are incorporated into Christ, whereby they have been baptized into his death so that they may also be raised with him (6:4). Paul's reference to baptism speaks of the washing away of sins that occurs at conversion. This experience of conversion is what Ezekiel prophesied in 36:25–28—namely that God would sprinkle clean water upon Israel, cleansing his people from all their sin, and that they would be given a new heart and spirit so to walk in righteousness. Paul says this reality of experiencing eschatological resurrection is sure in Christ because they are "united with him" (6:5).

Paul establishes this concept of union with Christ in Romans 5 when he says believers are no longer in Adam, but rather they are in Christ. Being united to the last Adam, death and sin no longer reign over the believer. Instead, "they have been liberated from the power of sin and transferred into the realm of righteousness."[24] As Paul says in 6:4, believers are able to "walk in newness of life" (ἡμεῖς ἐν καινότητι ζωῆς περιπατήσωμεν) because they share in Christ's resurrection. Here Beale notes that Paul employs new creation language through the use of καινότης, which is a cognate of καινος.[25] In both 2 Corinthians 5:17 and Galatians 6:15, καινος is used for "the well-known inaugurated eschatological expression 'new creation,' where in both cases it refers to resurrection life."[26] What Paul says in Romans 6:4-5 could be interpreted that believers will only experience resurrection in the future. However, in verses 11 and 13, it is clear that Paul envisions present resurrection. What Paul has said in verses 4-10 serves as the basis for believers to consider themselves "alive to God in Christ Jesus" (6:11) and to present themselves "to God as those who have been brought from death to life" (6:13).[27] In other words, the OT promise to Israel of eschatological resurrection and deliverance from exile has been inaugurated in Christ, and now is being experienced among the new Israel.

This participation in the promised resurrection is further demonstrated in Romans 7:4-6, where Paul says believers belong to Christ, "who has been raised from the dead, in order that we may bear fruit for God" (7:4), and serve "in the new way of the Spirit" (7:6). Again, Paul employs new creation language borrowed from Ezekiel 36:26, where God promised to give Israel "a new spirit" (cf. Jer 31:31-34).[28] Just as Paul explained in chapter 6, so here he reiterates that believers are

---

24. Schreiner, *Romans*, 298.

25. Beale, *New Testament Biblical Theology*, 251.

26. Ibid.

27. Moo, *Romans*, 367.

28. Dunn, *Romans 1-8*, 366.

no longer under the dominion of the old age, which is passing away. Instead, since they are joined to Christ, the last Adam, they experience the powers of the new age.[29]

The themes of resurrection and new exodus restoration are most strongly expressed in Romans 8. In 8:1–11, Paul again closely associates the Spirit with life. Beale helpfully points out, "Ezek. 37:5 is the only passage in the law that makes the same linkage in an eschatological context."[30] When Paul speaks of "life," he likely means resurrection life. In Ezekiel 37, the Spirit of the Lord was the instrument whereby Israel's resurrection would be accomplished (37:5–6, 9–10, 14). In Romans Paul sees this eschatological promise occurring in the Church; as he notes in 8:10, with the presence of the Spirit "believers will not be saddled with their weak and corruptible bodies forever."[31] The Spirit is life-giving and assures believers that they will overcome death through the resurrection of their bodies. Paul says that the reason "the Spirit is life" is "because of righteousness" (8:10). Paul refers here to God's saving righteousness demonstrated by the work of Christ on the cross. God, for his own righteousness' sake, will give life in Christ. This truth is consistent with the Jewish expectation that God would resurrect his people to vindicate his own name.[32]

Furthermore, in 8:11, Paul grounds the certainty of believers' resurrection in Christ's resurrection by the Spirit. It is because Christ is the true Israel that the promises of God find their fulfillment in him. Therefore, because Christ has been raised, so will all those who belong to him. Since the

---

29. Cranfield, *Romans*, 1:340; Schreiner, *Romans*, 352.

30. Beale, *New Testament Biblical Theology*, 253.

31. Schreiner, *Romans*, 414.

32. Kirk, *Unlocking Romans*, 16.

resurrection is tied to Israel's new exodus, it is not surprising that in 8:14–17, those united to Christ and who participate in his resurrection are also adopted as God's sons. They become his children and his heirs (8:17). Within the OT, the idea of "inheritance" was associated with the land (Deut 30:5; Num 34:2); the promises made to Abraham's offspring (Gen 15:7; 17:8); and the promise of restoration after exile (Isa 60:21; Ezek 36:8–12).[33] However, later Jewish writings seemed to expand the idea of "inheritance" to describe the eschatological life (*Pss. Sol.* 14:10; *1 Enoch* 40:9; 4 Macc 18:3).[34] Therefore, for Paul, the "inheritance" is likely the fulfillment of the OT promises realized in the new creation. If so, Christians are God's new creation people who inherit these promises.

Continuing on to 8:18–23, we see that the resurrection coincides with a new creation. Here Paul links the future resurrection and redemption of the body with the resurrection of the creation. As already established, the new creation was promised to Israel (Isa 65:17; 66:22), but Paul sees this promise belonging to the Church, the new Israel. Throughout chapters 6–8, Paul has argued this reality—namely that "Christians … [are] to be the actual beginning fulfillment of the prophesied spiritual resurrection of Israel that was to transpire in the latter days at the time of their restoration from exile."[35] Even though there is yet to be a full realization of these promises in the future, Paul understands the blessings of the new age to have invaded the present by virtue of Christ's resurrection from the dead.

---

33. Moo, *Romans*, 505.
34. Ibid., 505n45.
35. Beale, *New Testament Biblical Theology*, 254.

Salvation

The good news of Jesus' death and resurrection "is the power of God for salvation to everyone who believes" (Rom 1:16). Salvation is a term which describes God's work of delivering his people. For Paul such salvation is primarily eschatological.[36] In Romans 5 Paul declared that "since ... we have now been justified by his blood, much more shall we be saved by him from the wrath of God" (Rom 5:9). Again, in verse 10, Paul says that since believers have been reconciled they "shall ... be saved by his life." In both verses Paul speaks of a future reality. The eschatological nature of salvation is also identified in Romans 10:9–11, where those who confess Jesus as Lord and believe on him with their hearts "will be saved" (10:10). This understanding is reinforced in verse 11; Paul quotes Isaiah 28:16, which says, "Everyone who believes in him will not be put to shame." Paul does not view this as a present reality by which believers will no longer experience any shame—rather, this is an eschatological blessing of the coming age. Finally, Paul's future perspective of salvation is confirmed in Romans 13:11 when he says, "Salvation is nearer to us now than when we first believed."

Although fundamentally eschatological, we would be mistaken to assume that Paul limits salvation to the future. In Romans 8:24, Paul also sees salvation to be a past event: It is "in this hope we were saved." Since the coming age has invaded the present, salvation has an already-not-yet dimension. Nevertheless, the consummation of this promise is still in the future.

---

36. Schreiner, *Paul*, 225.

The eschatological salvation that Paul speaks of harkens back to the OT where Israel was promised salvation (Isa 1:27; 10:22; 12:2; 19:20; 30:15; 33:2; 35:4; 37:20; 45:17). In the OT God's promises of salvation were closely related to his righteousness.[37] This relationship is apparent by looking at Psalms and Isaiah where God's righteousness is found in conjunction with his salvation. For instance, Psalm 98:2–3 (Psa 97:2–3 LXX) says,

> The LORD has made known his salvation (σωτήριον); he has revealed his righteousness (δικαιοσύνην) in the sight of the nations. He has remembered his steadfast love and faithfulness to the house of Israel. All the ends of the earth have seen the salvation (σωτήριον) of our God.

In this passage, God's salvation being made known and his righteousness being revealed are closely related. The terminology is parallel—showing that God's righteousness is a saving righteousness.[38] This understanding is again illustrated in Isaiah 51:5–8:

> My righteousness (δικαιοσύνη) draws near,
>   my salvation (σωτήριόν) has gone out,
>   and my arms will judge the peoples;
> the coastlands hope for me,
>   and for my arm they wait.
> Lift up your eyes to the heavens,
>   and look at the earth beneath;

---

37. Mark A. Seifrid, *Christ, Our Righteousness: Paul's Theology of Justification*, New Studies in Biblical Theology 9 (Downers Grove, IL: InterVarsity Press, 2000), 39.
38. Schreiner, *Paul*, 198.

> for the heavens vanish like smoke,
>> the earth will wear out like a garment,
>> and they who dwell in it will die in like manner;
> but my salvation (σωτήριόν) will be forever,
>> and my righteousness (δικαιοσύνη) will never be
>> dismayed.

> "Listen to me, you who know righteousness,
>> the people in whose heart is my law;
> fear not the reproach of man,
>> nor be dismayed at their revilings.
> For the moth will eat them up like a garment,
>> and the worm will eat them like wool;
> but my righteousness (δικαιοσύνη) will be forever,
>> and my salvation (σωτήριόν) to all generations."

God's salvation for his people is linked to his righteousness
(see also Pss 31:1; 36:10; 40:10; 71:2; 88:10–12; 143:1; Isa 46:13).[39]

Paul makes this same connection in Romans 1:16–17, highlighting that the gospel "is the power of God for salvation" because "in it the righteousness of God is revealed." One could
say, in the resurrection of the crucified Christ, God's saving
act of righteousness is manifest; "God's righteousness is his
'vindicating act' of raising Christ from the dead *for* us. Here
the biblical themes of deliverance of the oppressed, his vindication of his Servant, his faithfulness to Israel and his salvation of the world are implicitly present."[40] Paul understands
that through the preached gospel, the OT promises of God's

---

39. Ibid.
40. Seifrid, *Christ, Our Righteousness*, 47.

mighty act of salvation for Israel have been made available for "everyone who believes" (Rom 1:16; cf. 3:21–24).

Redemption

Coinciding with salvation and deliverance is the concept of redemption (ἀπολύτρωσις). Although the term itself is not used more than twice (Rom 3:24; 8:23), the imagery of being set free from bondage is also found in Romans (6:15–23; cf. 7:2). The theme of redemption points back to the exodus, whereby Israel was set free from slavery in Egypt (Exod 6:6; 15:13; Deut 7:8; 9:26; 13:5; 15:15; 21:8; 24:18). The Prophet Isaiah wrote about a second, future exodus whereby God would fulfill his saving work in their lives (Isa 11:15–16; 40:3–11; 42:16; 43:1–19; 49:6–11; 51:10).[41] Isaiah's prophecies concerning this second exodus often use terminology of redemption (Isa 44:22, 23, 24; 51:11; 52:2; 62:12).[42]

It is these prophecies—in Isaiah, describing a new exodus—that Paul sees fulfilled in the redemption found in Christ. Even though these prophecies were partially fulfilled with Israel's return from Babylon, they were not fulfilled in their totality. Israel did not experience its sins being washed away, the indwelling Spirit, or the restoration of the cosmos. These elements have begun to be fulfilled through the redemption of Christ, and therefore should be described as "freedom from exile."[43]

---

41. Schreiner, *Paul*, 230.

42. G. K. Beale, "Colossians," in *Commentary on the New Testament Use of the Old Testament*, ed. G. K. Beale and D. A. Carson (Grand Rapids: Baker Academic, 2007), 848.

43. Schreiner, *Paul*, 230.

The freedom that Christ brings is from the power of sin. In Romans 3:24 Paul joins redemption with justification, because "in Christ" believers are "acquitted by God from all 'charges' that could be brought against [them] because of his or her sins."[44] Moreover, justification is said to be "free" (δωρεὰν) because it is based on the redemption that was provided by Christ. Because of Christ's sacrificial death and resurrection, believers "having been set free (ἐλευθερωθέντες) from sin, have become slaves (ἐδουλώθητε) of righteousness" (Rom 6:18). In Christ, believers are transferred from the power of sin and made subject to the power of righteousness, yet it was Israel who was promised deliverance from exile when their sins were forgiven and everlasting righteousness would reign (Dan 9:24). For Paul, this liberation from the power of sin fulfills the promises to Israel in the OT:[45] Those in Christ are experiencing the freedom of the new exodus and blessings of the new creation.

Christ redeemed believers not only from the power of sin, but also from the curse of the law (cf. Gal 3:13). Although Paul does not make use of ἀπολύτρωσις in Romans 7, the imagery of redemption is still there when he says, "But now we are released (κατηργήθημεν) from the law, having died to that which held (κατέχω) us captive" (Rom 7:6). To be held (κατέχω) by the law is another way to speak of being under the power of sin. It refers to the "state of Israel in the old age."[46] However, Paul says believers, through their identification with Christ, have died to the law (7:4) and now "serve in the new way of the

---

44. Moo, *Romans*, 227.

45. Schreiner, *Romans*, 334.

46. Schreiner, *Paul*, 231.

Spirit" (7:6).[47] Nevertheless, though the promises of the new exodus have become a reality for those in Christ, Paul understands that redemption is yet to be consummated. In Romans 8:23, he links the redemption of the body and the adoption of sons with the resurrection. At the resurrection, not only will believers have their bodies redeemed, but the entire creation will be renewed as well (8:20–21).

Summary

As we've seen, the theme of Israel's new exodus saturates Romans. With the preaching of the gospel, Paul declares that the promises of Israel's restoration have now come in Jesus Christ. In the OT, the promises of deliverance from exile and restoration were often associated with resurrection; Paul later preached the good news of Jesus' resurrection, which inaugurated the new exodus. Just as Jesus triumphed over sin and death through his resurrection, those who are united to him will share in a resurrection like his. The gospel of God's Son effects salvation for both Jew and Gentile, whereby they are redeemed from sin and the curse of the law. These are the promises that were to accompany Israel's new exodus. Therefore, Paul's theology of a new exodus has become a reality in Christ. Those identified with him are rightly understood as the new Israel, inheriting the promise of the new creation.

---

47. In Romans 7:6, Paul contrasts the "new way of the Spirit (πνεύματος)" with "the old way of the written code (γράμματος)." The γράμμα describes the old age ruled by the law, whereas πνεῦμα represents the arrival of the new age. See Bernardin Schneider, "The Meaning of St. Paul's Antithesis 'The Letter and the Spirit,' " *The Catholic Biblical Quarterly*, no. 15 (1953): 163–207; Ernst Käsemann, *Perspectives on Paul* (Philadelphia: Fortress Press, 1971), 143.

THE NEW COVENANT

In the OT, God's promises for Israel's restoration coincided with a new covenant (Jer 31:31-40). This covenant would not be like the old covenant that Israel broke (Jer 31:32). Rather, (1) God would write his law on their hearts (Jer 31:33); (2) everyone in the covenant community would have a saving knowledge of God (Jer 31:34a); and (3) God would forgive all their sins (Jer 31:34b). Although, the phrase "new covenant" is not used by Ezekiel, the same promise is made in Ezekiel 36:22-32. The Lord says that when Israel is restored he will cleanse the nation of all her sin (36:25), he will give them a new heart and place his Spirit within them so that they may obey the law (36:26-27), and they will be his people and he will be their God (36:28).

In the book of Romans, the Apostle Paul argues that the blessings of the new covenant are a present reality in the Church and are shared by both Jews and Gentiles. These blessings include:

a) the gift of the Spirit (Rom 2:29; 5:5; 7:6; 8:2, 4, 5, 6, 9, 10, 11, 14, 15, 16, 23, 26; 14:17; 15:13, 16, 19, 30; cf. Joel 2:28-29; Isa 44:3; Ezek 11:19; 36:26-27);

b) the circumcision of the heart (Rom 2:5, 29; cf. Jer 31:33; 32:39, 40; Ezek 11:19; 36:26, 27);

c) the ability to obey the law (Rom 2:26-27; 3:27-31; 8:1-4; 13:8-10; cf. Jer 31:33; Ezek 36:27); and

d) the forgiveness of sins whereby God's people would be justified (Rom 2:13; 3:24, 26, 28; 4:5, 6, 9 5:1, 9; 6:7; 8:30; 9:30; 10:10; cf. Isa 53:11; Jer 31:34; Ezek 36:25).

Since the promises of the new covenant are fulfilled in the Church, it is right to identify the Church as the new Israel.[48] Paul does not view the Church as merely partakers in the "spiritual blessings" of the new covenant.[49] Rather, the "already" aspect of these blessings is a guarantee of the inheritance to come (Rom 8:12–17, 23). Both Jews and Gentiles—having been united to Christ—are on equal footing, together inheriting all the promises of God.[50]

The Gift of the Spirit

In Romans Paul assures believers that they have a secure hope because "God's love has been poured into [their] hearts through the Holy Spirit who has been given to [them]" (5:5). This gift of the Spirit was to mark the new age promised to Israel in the OT (Joel 2:28–29; cf. Isa 44:3; Ezek 11:19; 36:26–27) and to enable Israel to be obedient to God's law. Paul says this reality has come in the Church, where the law is fulfilled among the Gentiles (Rom 2:26–27, 8:1–4). In fact, Paul goes so far as to say that those who have the Spirit are true Jews (2:29).

Again, union with Christ allows believers to enter into the realm where righteousness and life reign (5:17). Subsequently in 7:1–6, Paul can say that those who are united to Christ are

---

48. Hans K. LaRondelle, *The Israel of God in Prophecy: Principles of Prophetic Interpretation*, Andrews University Monographs v. 13 (Berrien Springs, MI: Andrews University Press, 1983), 121.

49. Contra Vlach, who says, "The new covenant also has an 'already/not yet' aspect to it in regard to the manner of its fulfillment. Spiritual aspects of the new covenant such as forgiveness of sins and the indwelling Holy Spirit are being realized in the present era while the physical blessings of the covenant await a future fulfillment with national Israel" (Vlach, *Has the Church Replaced Israel*, 158).

50. Contra Bruce Ware, who suggests that the nation of Israel will receive distinguishable promises distinct from the Church (Bruce A. Ware, "The New Covenant and the People(s) of God," in *Dispensationalism, Israel, and the Church: The Search for Definition* [Grand Rapids: Zondervan, 1992], 96–97).

now in the new era of the Spirit as opposed to the old era of the law—believers "are released from the law, having died to that which held us captive, so that we serve in the new way of the Spirit and not in the old way of the written code." The "new way of the Spirit" fulfills the old covenant promise that Israel would one day be able to keep the law.

Moreover, Paul assures believers that they will experience the redemption of their bodies and adoption as sons because they have the "firstfruits of the Spirit" (8:23). The imagery of firstfruits is a metaphor borrowed from the OT recalling how Israel, by faith, was to offer up the firstfruits of its crops to God and trust that he would supply the harvest. In the same way, the Spirit is the firstfruit guaranteeing the full realization of the age to come.[51]

Circumcision of the Heart

Along with the gift of the Spirit, God promised to circumcise the hearts of his people so that they may obey his statutes (Jer 31:33; 32:39, 40; Ezek 11:19; 36:26, 27). In Romans 2:25-29, Paul contends that with the arrival of the new covenant, physical circumcision no longer marks off the people of God. Such an assertion is a "radical reevaluation of the covenant," for the covenantal sign of circumcision was of utmost importance to the Jew.[52] Keeping with the command given to Abraham in Genesis 17:9-14, it would be unthinkable that any Jew would abstain from circumcision. After all, the Lord himself said to Abraham, "Any uncircumcised male who is not circumcised in the flesh of his foreskin shall be cut off from his people; he

---

51. Kaylor, *Paul's Covenant Community*, 151.
52. Schreiner, *Romans*, 138.

has broken my covenant" (Gen 17:14). Therefore, in the mind of the Jew, to be circumcised marked one off as part of the covenant people of God.

In Romans 2:25–27, Paul combats the idea that physical circumcision guarantees acceptance in the people of God. He says circumcision only has salvific value if one keeps the whole law. Startlingly, Paul says that for Jews who transgress the law, "[their] circumcision becomes uncircumcision" (2:25)—they are not regarded as the people of God. However, for Gentiles who keep the law, their uncircumcision will be counted (λογισθήσεται) as circumcision (2:26). These Gentiles are then regarded as the true members of the Abrahamic covenant.

Paul gives the reason for this in Romans 2:28–29: True "circumcision [is not] outward and physical ... [it] is a matter of the heart, by the Spirit (πνεῦμα), not by the letter (γράμμα)." Paul contrasts circumcision of the flesh (2:28b) with circumcision of the heart (2:29b). Even in the OT, God called his people to be circumcised in heart (Lev 26:41; Deut 10:16; Jer 4:4; 9:26). The OT also looked forward to a day when God would circumcise the hearts of his people (Deut 30:6; cf. Ezek 36:26). However, the fulfillment of this promise would not come until God made a new covenant (Jer 31:31–34). In the new covenant, God would write his law on the hearts of his people so that all may obey his commands. The Prophet Ezekiel explains that this obedience will not come until God replaces their dead hearts and gives them his Spirit (Ezek 36:26–27).

The Jews would have been looking to the day when God would perform this heart change.[53] Yet the Jews did not expect that physical circumcision would no longer be required

53. Moo, *Romans*, 174.

to enter into the people of God.[54] Nonetheless, this change is precisely what happened, for the "uncircumcised" Gentiles "who keep the law" will be considered circumcised on the last day (Rom 2:26). The Gentiles of whom Paul speaks have received the blessings of the new covenant—namely, the gift of the Spirit and the circumcision of their hearts (2:29). And this letter-Spirit antithesis in Romans 2:29 is an "eschatological distinction."[55] The circumcision of the heart cannot come through the old covenant of the law (i.e., the letter). Rather, it must come in the newness of the Spirit (cf. Rom 7:6).[56]

The Fulfillment of the Law

With the arrival of the Spirit, God promised to circumcise the hearts of his people so that they may keep his law (Ezek 36:26–37; cf. Jer 31:33). As seen in Romans 2:25–29, Paul argues that this new covenant promise has already become a reality for Gentile Christians.[57] Again, in 6:17, Paul gives thanks

---

54. Schreiner, *Romans*, 141–42.

55. Brendan Byrne, *Romans*, Sacra Pagina 6 (Collegeville, MN: Liturgical Press, 1996), 104.

56. Moo says, "The ἐν in this phrase could be instrumental - the circumcision is accomplished 'by' the Spirit - but this meaning does not fit well with the other object of the preposition: γράμματι. It is preferable, therefore, to think that it denotes sphere" (Moo, *Romans*, 175n45). However, Käsemann is probably correct to suggest that a decision over whether the ἐν should be viewed instrumentally or locally "is relatively unimportant" (Käsemann, *Perspectives on Paul*, 146). Paul most likely has both ideas in mind. Heart circumcision is "by" the work of the Spirit and "in" the new age of the Spirit.

57. Contra Paul J. Achtemeier, *Romans*, Interpretation (Atlanta: John Knox Press, 1985), 51–53; John Calvin, *Commentaries on the Epistle of Paul the Apostle to the Romans*, trans. John Owen, Calvin's Commentaries (Grand Rapids: Baker Books, 2009), 110; Joseph A. Fitzmyer, *Romans: A New Translation with Introduction and Commentary*, The Anchor Bible 33 (New York: Doubleday, 1993), 322; Ernst Käsemann, *Commentary on Romans* (Grand Rapids: Eerdmans, 1980), 73; Moo, *Romans*, 169–71; Frank Thielman, *Paul & the Law: A Contextual Approach* (Downers Grove, IL: InterVarsity Press, 1994), 174. For a defense that Paul views these Gentiles as

to God for the Romans who are no longer "slaves of sin" but have become "obedient from the heart."[58] This heartfelt obedience harkens back to Paul's statement in Romans 1:5 of his apostolic commissioning to bring about "the obedience of faith ... among all the nations" (cf. 15:18). The reason Paul is able to call the nations to obedience in Christ is because the new age of the Spirit has been inaugurated.

That the new age has dawned is made explicit in 8:1-11. In this passage Paul states that "the righteous requirement of the law" is now fulfilled among those who are "in Christ" and who "walk ... according to the Spirit" (8:1-4). Furthermore, there is "now no condemnation" (8:1). This use of the adverb "now" (νῦν) "signals a new era of salvation history, one in which God's covenantal promises are being fulfilled, when his people are enjoying the freedom from condemnation God promised."[59] With the dawn of the new age, "the law of the Spirit of life has set [believers] free in Christ Jesus from the law of sin and death" (8:2). This freedom is made possible by the atoning sacrifice of God's Son, Jesus Christ (8:3). As we saw in chapter 2 of this book, "Son" is a reference to Israel, thus identifying Jesus as the true Israel. For Paul, those who

---

Christians, see Cranfield, *Romans*, 1:173; A. Andrew Das, *Paul, the Law, and the Covenant* (Peabody, MA: Hendrickson Publishers, 2001), 184-86; Dunn, *Romans 1-8*, 233-35; Simon J. Gathercole, *Where Is Boasting?: Early Jewish Soteriology and Paul's Response in Romans 1-5* (Grand Rapids: Eerdmans, 2002), 127-29; Thomas R. Schreiner, "Did Paul Believe in Justification by Works? Another Look at Romans 2," *Bulletin for Biblical Research*, no. 3 (1993): 148-49; N. T. Wright, "The Law in Romans 2," in *Paul and the Mosaic Law*, ed. James D. G. Dunn (Grand Rapids: Eerdmans, 2001), 134-36.

58. Frank Thielman, "The Story of Israel and the Theology of Romans 5-8," in *Pauline Theology*, ed. David M. Hay and E. Elizabeth Johnson, Society of Biblical Literature Symposium Series 23 (Atlanta: Society of Biblical Literature, 2002), 187-88.

59. Schreiner, *Romans*, 397.

are identified with the true Israel share in the blessings of the new covenant made to Israel. Christ's work on the cross serves as the foundation for the "transformative work of the Spirit."[60]

Paul describes the work of the Spirit in Romans 8:5–8: "Those who live according to the Spirit set their minds on the things of the Spirit" (8:5b). This Spirit-led life contrasts with those who live according to the flesh (8:5a). Paul says that those who live according to the flesh will die (8:6) because they are unable to submit to the law of God (8:7). However, those who have the Spirit receive the blessing of "life and peace" (8:6) because they do what the law commands and so please God (8:7–8). Paul's theology as explained in 8:1–11 serves as the basis for later exhortations in Romans. For example, in 13:8–10, Paul exhorts believers to love one another (13:8a). The one who loves, Paul says, "has fulfilled the law" (13:8b). He then substantiates his claim by quoting from the law of Moses, showing that all the commandments "are summed up in this word: 'You shall love your neighbor as yourself' " (13:9).

What is evident from these passages is that the new covenant promise to Israel—namely, that the law would be kept through the work of the Spirit—is fulfilled in the Church. Paul argues that those who find their identity in God's Son, the true Israel, have been given the Spirit and so are enabled to keep the law. They are then pleasing to God (8:8) and experience the promised life and peace of the age to come (8:6). It is these who keep the law, who are rightly a part of God's new covenant people, the new Israel.

---

60. Schreiner, *Paul*, 264.

The Forgiveness of Sins

Another blessing of the new covenant is that God would forgive Israel's sins and cleanse his people from all their iniquities
(Jer 31:34; Ezek 36:25, 33). Surprisingly, in Romans Paul does
not speak specifically of believers having their sins forgiven.
Instead, he uses the language of "counted as righteousness"
(Rom 4:5). Paul links this language with forgiveness in 4:7–8,
where he cites Psalm 32:1–2, "Blessed are those whose lawless
deeds are forgiven, and whose sins are covered; blessed is the
man against whom the Lord will not count his sin."

Righteousness (δικαιοσύνη) is primarily a forensic term for
Paul, and speaks of God's saving righteousness, which is made
available by faith (1:17).[61] The forensic nature of righteousness
is more clearly seen through Paul's use of the verb δικαιόω.
For example, in 3:28, Paul says, "For we hold that one is justified
(δικαιοῦσθαι) by faith apart from works of the law" (cf. 3:20, 24,
26, 30; 5:1).[62] If righteousness comes by faith, and not through
the works of the law, then God judiciously declares believers
to be vindicated from all their sin (cf. 6:7).

This vindication from sin is what Paul articulates in 4:5
when he says, "And to the one who does not work but believes in him who justifies (δικαιοῦντα) the ungodly, his faith
is counted (λογίζεται) as righteousness (δικαιοσύνην)." It is
within the context of justification that Paul then cites Psalm
32:1–2, which speaks of forgiveness of sin (4:6–8). Therefore,
Paul pictures a close relationship between righteousness

---

61. The limitations of this work prevent discussion over whether righteousness
should be understood as covenant faithfulness. For a defense of the forensic view
of righteousness, see Schreiner, *Paul*, 189–217; Seifrid, *Christ, Our Righteousness*.
62. Schreiner, *Paul*, 204.

and forgiveness (cf. 4:25).[63] This close relationship is further evidenced through Paul's use of λογίζομαι. This term means "to reckon" or "count" and is used in a law-court setting.[64] In Paul's theology, God, the judge, counts sinners as righteous through faith in Jesus.

To be declared righteous, then, is to have your sins forgiven, to be identified as a benefit of the new covenant. Paul says elsewhere that "since we have been justified by faith, we have peace with God through our Lord Jesus Christ" (5:1). Peace was an eschatological gift promised to Israel in the OT whereby God would fulfill his covenant promise (Isa 9:6–7; 32:15–17; 48:20–22; 54:10; Mic 5:4–5; Hag 2:9; Zech 8:12).[65] Ezekiel speaks of the new covenant as a "covenant of peace" (Ezek 34:25; 37:26), where his people would be led by the future Davidic king (34:23–31; 37:24–28; cf. Isa 9:6–7; Mic 5:4–5).[66] Paul writes that through Christ (Rom 5:1), the Davidic king (1:3), the Church has the forgiveness of sins and now is at peace with God in the new covenant (1:7; 8:6; 14:17; 15:13).

Another means by which Paul expresses the idea of forgiveness is the reconciliation of believers to God (5:10, 11; 11:15). When Paul speaks of reconciliation, he has in mind the OT restoration promises of the prophets (Isa 49:18–26; 61:1; Ezek 37:1–14; 39:29).[67] Both Isaiah and Ezekiel present the restoration of Israel as coinciding with God establishing his "covenant of peace" (Isa 54:10; Ezek 34:25; 37:26).[68] Paul understands

---

63. Ibid.
64. H. W. Bartsch, "λογίζομαι," in Horst Robert Balz and Gerhard Schneider, *Exegetical Dictionary of the New Testament*, vol. 2 (Grand Rapids: Eerdmans, 1990), 354.
65. Schreiner, *Romans*, 253.
66. Ibid.
67. Thielman, "The Story of Israel and the Theology of Romans 5–8," 178.
68. Ibid., 178.

the basis of believers' reconciliation with God to be that they "have now been justified by [Jesus'] blood" (5:9). Since justification is linked with forgiveness (4:5–8), it is not a stretch to see reconciliation as also closely related.

While it is true that in Romans Paul does not use the language of "forgiveness of sins," it by no means suggests that he does not view forgiveness as a reality for believers. Rather, the new covenant blessing of forgiveness is presented in the themes of "justification," "having peace with God," and "being reconciled to God."

Summary

Paul argues that the new covenant promise to Israel is now realized in the Church. In Christ, believers experience the indwelling of the Holy Spirit. The Spirit has circumcised their hearts so that they are now able to keep the law. Through faith, believers do not have their sin counted against them—God has justified them. All of these blessings were promised to OT Israel. Therefore, those who are recipients of these promises are rightly identified as the new Israel in Christ.

THE ABRAHAMIC COVENANT

Within the storyline of Scripture, the covenant God made with Abraham "stands in contrast to the judgments of God on human sin and presents anew the plan of creation."[69] From the OT we see God promising Abraham a great name, a multitude of offspring, a land to dwell in, a relationship with the covenant God, and that, through his offspring, the nations

---

69. Gentry and Wellum, *Kingdom Through Covenant*, 630.

would be blessed (Gen 12:1–3; 15:4–5; 17:1–8; 18:18–19; 22:16–18).[70] In light of God's promise in Genesis 3:15, the Abrahamic covenant is the means "by which God will fulfill his promises for humanity (universal, creation focus, which drives us forward to the new covenant)."[71] Wright describes the Abrahamic covenant thus: "Abraham emerges within the structure of Genesis as the answer to the plight of all humankind. The line of disaster and of the 'curse', from Adam, through Cain, through the Flood to Babel, begins to be reversed when God calls Abraham and says 'in you shall all the families of the earth be blessed.' "[72]

In Romans, the Abrahamic covenant is shown as fulfilled in the Church through faith in Jesus Christ (Rom 4:24–25). With the inauguration of the new covenant, the blessings of the Abrahamic covenant are being realized as both Jews and Gentiles exercise a faith like that of Abraham (4:11–12). As a result, the blessing of forgiveness is made for all nations (4:6–9), and Abraham's children have become heirs of the world (4:13).[73]

All the Nations are Blessed

From the outset of Romans, Paul has made it clear that the gospel is the good news of salvation for all nations (1:16; cf. 1:5, 13; 3:29; 4:17–24; 9:24, 30; 11:11, 12, 13, 25; 15:9–12, 16, 18, 27; 16:26). Paul contends that through faith in Christ, the people of God have now expanded to all the nations. As a result, the promise that in Abraham's offspring all the nations will be blessed is coming to pass (Gen 12:3; Isa 19:18–25; 49:6; Dan 7:14, 27). For Paul, the blessing that was promised to Abraham

---

70. Ibid., 630–31.

71. Ibid., 631.

72. Wright, *The New Testament and the People of God*, 262.

73. Kaylor, *Paul's Covenant Community*, 89–90.

and his offspring is "the blessing of forgiveness which is pronounced upon both the circumcised and the uncircumcised (Rom 4:6-9)."[74] This inclusion of the uncircumcised is consistent with what Paul teaches in Romans 2:25-29: that physical circumcision no longer marks off the people of God. Therefore, it is essential for Paul's readers to understand that since the basis of becoming a true child of Abraham is through faith in Christ, then Jews and Gentiles must be equally a part of Abraham's family.

Heirs of the World

Paul also says that, as children of Abraham, believers have become heirs of the world (4:13-16). Even though the Hebrew Scriptures do not include an explicit statement that Abraham and his children would be heirs of the world, the OT does suggest this to be the case (Pss 2:7-12; 22:27-28; 47:7-9; 72:8-11, 17; Isa 2:1-4; 19:18-25; 49:6-7; 52:7-10; 55:3-5; 66:23; Amos 9:11-12; Zeph 3:9-10; Zech 14:9).[75] Beale observes that "the rationale underlying Paul's worldwide view is most probably the various OT texts ... in which Israel's promise of the land was viewed to concern the whole world."[76] Paul identifies this inheritance to be a new creation (8:16-25). Therefore, Paul sees the fulfillment of the Abrahamic covenant to be joined with the promises of a new creation. These promises were originally given to OT Israel; however, being fulfilled in the true Israel, these promises are mediated to all by faith.

---

74. Ibid., 89.
75. Schreiner, *Romans*, 227.
76. Beale, *New Testament Biblical Theology*, 757.

Summary

As we've just seen, God's saving promises to Israel concerning a new creation have been inaugurated in Christ and are experienced in the Church through union with him. Paul declares the promises of Israel's eschatological restoration have now been inaugurated with the resurrection of Jesus Christ; therefore, Paul preached the good news of God's deliverance whereby salvation and redemption are made available for not only the Jews, but also the Gentiles. In light of this, we can see that the new covenant promise to Israel is now being realized in the Church. In Christ believers experience the new covenant blessing that the Holy Spirit would take residence in their hearts. As a result, the Spirit has cleansed believers from all their iniquities and has circumcised their hearts, so that they are now able to keep the law of God. Finally, with the inauguration of the new covenant, Paul stresses that the promises to Abraham are also being fulfilled. Through faith in Christ, both Jews and Gentiles become children of Abraham and heirs of the world.

CHAPTER 4

Israelite Language Applied to the Church

With Israel's promises being present realities in the Church, Paul proclaims that this new community in Christ is the new Israel. Through Christ, Gentiles have been made coheirs of these promises, eagerly awaiting the eschatological hope in the glory of God with the saints of old. No wonder, then, that Paul applies OT Israelite language to the Church. Since the Church is rightful heir of God's saving promises of a new creation, then it follows that the Church bears the titles of God's true people, the new Israel.

Vlach has argued that applying Israelite imagery to the Church only shows that "believing Jews and Gentiles compose the one people of God in a salvation sense. But that this truth does not rule out a future role for national Israel or indicate that the church is now Israel."[1] However, to argue that the

---

1. Michael J. Vlach, *Has the Church Replaced Israel? A Theological Evaluation* (Nashville: B&H Academic, 2010), 156.

unity of Jews and Gentiles is only in a "salvation sense" does not support the idea that the nation of Israel retains a distinct and privileged position in the future. As we've already discussed, the promise of salvation is linked with Israel's restoration promises. Paul does not portion out the rest of the OT promises to be reserved for the nation of Israel. Rather, he argues that "in Christ" both Jews and Gentiles are rightful recipients of all God's promises. Nevertheless, Paul does not present the Church as a "replacement" of Israel, but as "the continuation of Israel into the new age."[2]

In the chapter to follow, we'll discover: Paul does apply Israelite language to the Church, because it is in the Church where the OT promises find their fulfillment.[3] These promises, which were at one time only available for believing Jews, have now expanded to include the Gentiles through faith in the true Israel, Jesus. Because the Church is united to Jesus, "it is important to maintain that the church is not merely like Israel, but actually is Israel."[4] This designation will become clearer as attention is given to the specific Israelite imagery Paul employs while speaking of the believers in Romans.

---

2. Douglas J. Moo, *The Epistle to the Romans*, New International Commentary on the New Testament (Grand Rapids: Eerdmans, 1996), 709.

3. For much of this chapter, I am indebted to the work of Charles D. Provan, *The Church Is Israel Now: The Transfer of Conditional Privilege* (Vallecito, CA: Ross House, 2003). Although I do not see as much continuity between the Church and Israel as Provan does, the survey of Israelite imagery applied to the Church has been helpful nevertheless.

4. G. K. Beale, *A New Testament Biblical Theology: The Unfolding of the Old Testament in the New* (Grand Rapids: Baker Academic, 2011), 653. Contra Robert L. Saucy, *The Case for Progressive Dispensationalism: The Interface Between Dispensational & Non-Dispensational Theology* (Grand Rapids: Zondervan, 1993), 189.

The Titles for Believers

Church

Surprisingly, in Romans Paul does not use the term "church" (ἐκκλησία) until the last chapter. However, it would be a mistake to conclude that he does not view the Roman Christians as part of the Church. In 16:3 Paul sends greetings to Prisca and Aquilla, hosts of a house church in Rome (16:5). Paul refers to other Christian assemblies as the "church" (16:1, 4, 16). The greetings Paul offers are a demonstration of the love that all those who belong to the Lord share.[5] This common love among all the churches is the basis for why Paul concludes his greeting with "All the churches of Christ greet you" (16:16). Paul views the local church in Rome to be united with the universal Church abroad.

It is the "church" (ἐκκλησία) that Paul identifies as this new covenant community of Jews and Gentiles who have come to faith in Christ. Why does Paul use this term to describe God's people? The answer does not lie in the etymology of the word ἐκ-καλεω ("called out"). While believers are those who are "called" and "elect," Paul does not use ἐκκλησία because it directly indicates such realities.[6] Rather, Paul draws upon the term "church" (ἐκκλησία) from the old-covenant community of Israel: The OT regularly refers to Israel as the "assembly of the Lord" (קְהַל יְהוָה, cf. Num 16:3; 20:4; Deut 23:1, 8; 1 Chr 28:8). It is not insignificant, then, that elsewhere, Paul uses the

---

5. Robert L. Saucy, *The Case for Progressive Dispensationalism: The Interface Between Dispensational & Non-Dispensational Theology* (Grand Rapids: Zondervan, 1993), 189.
6. James D. G. Dunn, *The Theology of Paul the Apostle* (Grand Rapids: Eerdmans, 1998), 537.

phrase "church of God" (1 Cor 1:2; 10:32; 11:22; 2 Cor 1:1; 1 Thess 2:14). In Romans 16:16, Paul uses a parallel phrase, "the churches of Christ." This phrase may imply "continuity with 'the assembly of Yahweh,' without causing confusion over who 'the Lord' might be when speaking of 'the assembly of the Lord.' "[7] Consequently, there is "little doubt that Paul intended to depict the little assemblies of Christian believers as equal manifestations of and in direct continuity with 'the assembly of Yahweh,' 'the assembly of Israel.' "[8] In other words, Paul presents the Church to be the new people of God, the new Israel.[9]

Called

Just as Israel was "called" ($\kappa\alpha\lambda\dot{\epsilon}\omega$ [Isa 41:9; 42:6; 43:1; 45:3; 48:12; 51:2]), so Paul says that the Church has been called ($\kappa\lambda\eta\tau\dot{o}\varsigma$; $\kappa\alpha\lambda\dot{\epsilon}\omega$ [Rom 1:6, 7; 8:28, 30; 9:24, 25, 26]). Note that Paul identifies the Church as those "called to belong to Jesus Christ" (1:6). Here again, Paul pictures the Church as united to the true Israel. This union serves as the basis for why Paul can call the Church "saints" (1:7), "my people" (9:25a), "beloved" (9:25b), and "sons of the living God" (9:26). It is this calling by which God has chosen a people for his own possession, just as when he called Israel out of Egypt.

---

7. Ibid., 538.

8. Ibid.

9. See Rudolf Bultmann, *Theology of the New Testament* (London: SCM Press, 1952), 39; George E. Ladd, *A Theology of the New Testament* (Grand Rapids: Eerdmans, 1993), 582; Herman Ridderbos, *Paul: An Outline of His Theology* (Grand Rapids: Eerdmans, 1997), 328; Frank Thielman, *Theology of the New Testament: A Canonical and Synthetic Approach* (Grand Rapids: Zondervan, 2005), 708; Thomas R. Schreiner, *Paul, Apostle of God's Glory in Christ: A Pauline Theology* (Downers Grove, IL: InterVarsity Press, 2006), 332.

Saints

In the OT Israel was to be a holy (ἅγιος) nation (Exod 19:6 LXX; cf. Deut 7:6; 14:2, 21; 28:29). Here in Romans, Paul also calls the Church "saints" (1:7; 8:27; 12:13; 15:25, 26, 31: 16:2, 15). However, the most likely background for Paul's usage of "saints" is from Daniel 7. As shown earlier, in chapter 2, the vision in Daniel 7 speaks of the coming messianic figure, the "Son of Man," whereby he will receive the eschatological kingdom, all peoples will serve him, and he will exercise dominion forever (Dan 7:13–14). But in Daniel 7:18, as the vision is interpreted, the reader notes that "the saints of the Most High shall receive the kingdom and possess the kingdom forever, forever, and ever" (cf. Dan 7:22). The relationship between the "Son of Man" and the "saints" both receiving the kingdom can be explained by what some refer to as "the one and the many" or "corporate representation," where a kingdom, nation or family is represented by a king, priest or father.[10] In Daniel 7, the Son of Man represents the nation of Israel, in whom they are summed up.

This concept of union with the Messiah is an idea that Paul emphasizes in Romans (6:11, 23; 8:1, 2, 39; 12:5). In a similar manner to Jesus' self-identification as Daniel's "Son of Man" (Matt 24:30; Mark 13:26), Paul speaks of those who are united to Christ as the eschatological saints. Therefore, the hope that Israel would receive God's everlasting kingdom finds its fulfillment in the Church, the end-time "saints of the most high" (Dan 7:22). Further, Paul sees the saints in Rome as recipients of God's kingdom in Romans 14:17, where he expounds upon

---

10. Beale, *New Testament Biblical Theology*, 192.

the kingdom ethic—an ethic that is characterized by the new creation blessings "of righteousness and peace and joy in the Holy Spirit." Again, such a conclusion does not advocate that the Church has replaced Israel. Rather, Paul understands that the saints of kingdom consist of both believing Jews and Gentiles.

Beloved

In Christ, Paul also calls the Church God's "beloved" (1:7; 9:22–25; 12:19; 16:5, 8, 9, 12). The title "beloved" is frequently applied to Israel in the OT (Deut 32:15; 33:12; Isa 44:2; Jer 11:15; 12:7; Pss 60:5 [59:7 LXX]; 108:6 [107:7 LXX]).[11] Notably, in Romans 9:25–26, Paul calls Christians God's beloved: "Those who were not my people I will call 'my people,' and her who was not beloved I will call 'beloved.' And in the very place where it was said to them, 'You are not my people' there they will be called 'sons of the living God." Paul cites Hosea 2:23 and 1:10, two texts regarding the future salvation and restoration of Israel. However, Paul applies these texts to the salvation of Gentiles.[12] That Paul has Gentiles in mind is clear in the previous verse: "even us whom he has called, not from the Jews only but also from the Gentiles" (9:24).

Vlach objects to this interpretation, suggesting that Paul is merely quoting Hosea to show that "God's electing purposes for Gentiles is [sic] parallel or analogous to God's choosing Israel."[13] However, Moo aptly notes, "Paul requires more than an analogy to establish from Scripture justification for God's

---

11. Ibid., 669.
12. Contra John A. Battle, Jr., "Paul's Use of the Old Testament in Romans 9:25–26," *Grace Theological Journal* 2 (1982): 115–29.
13. Vlach, *Has the Church Replaced Israel*, 103.

calling of Gentiles to be his people."[14] It is not enough to argue that Paul's use of "as indeed" (ὡς καὶ) in 9:25 is an indication of analogy and not fulfillment. In Romans 9:29 Paul uses an equivalent grammatical construction (καὶ καθὼς, "and just as") to introduce the initial fulfillment of Isaiah's prophesy that only a remnant of Israel would be saved. Furthermore, Paul not only applies Hosea to believing Gentiles, but also to believing Jews (9:24). Therefore, "to say that somehow the prophecy is fulfilled by Jews and merely analogically applied to gentiles would be a convoluted and inconsistent conclusion."[15] Instead, Paul understood both Jews and Gentiles through faith in Christ as constituting the inaugural fulfillment of Hosea 1–2.

Earlier in Romans, Paul opened the door for non-Jews to be considered part of Israel (cf. Rom 2:25–29). He continues this direction in 9:6, where he says, "For not all who are descended from Israel belong to Israel." Even though Paul speaks of a distinction between ethnic Israelites, he has opened up the possibility for Gentiles to be a part of the Israel of promise without becoming ethnic Israelites (9:7–8).[16] Paul's presupposition that Gentiles have become part of Israel through faith is substantiated by the context of Hosea 1:10; Hosea 1:11 reads, "And the children of Judah and the children of Israel shall be

---

14. Douglas J. Moo, *The Epistle to the Romans*, New International Commentary on the New Testament (Grand Rapids: Eerdmans, 1996), 613.

15. Beale, *New Testament Biblical Theology*, 706.

16. Dunn concurs, "By switching terms to 'Israel,' however Paul opened up a different possibility. For if the function of 'Israel' as a name is to identify primarily by relation to God and to God's choice, and not by differentiation from other nations and race, then the issue of whether Gentiles can be included may be resolved on a quite different basis. Strictly speaking, it is not possible to include 'Greek' within 'Jews'; that is simply a confusion of identifiers. But it might be possible to include 'Gentiles' within 'Israel' and this in effect is what Paul attempts to do in Romans 9–11 (Dunn, *The Theology of Paul the Apostle*, 506). Contra Eastman, "Israel and the Mercy of God," 382; Wagner, *Heralds of the Good News*, 49–51.

gathered together, and they shall appoint for themselves one head." Israel's restoration will come about as it is led by its covenant "head."[17] There is little doubt that this "head" is the future Davidic king who is spoken of in Hosea 3:5: "Afterward the children of Israel shall return and seek the LORD their God, and David their king, and they shall come in fear to the LORD and to his goodness in the latter days." Beale describes the significance of this context as Paul applies Hosea to believing Gentiles:

> Paul's contextual purview likely included the notion of a messianic deliverer who would lead the restoration, with whom end-time Israel would be identified. Paul's application of the prophecy, not only to Jews but also to gentiles, suggests that he sees gentiles to be identified with this messianic leader, which the OT and NT elsewhere identify as an individual representative for eschatological Israel.[18]

If so, this example of corporate representation is consistent with what we have already examined in favor of Jesus is the true Israel and Davidic king, in whom the new Israel is defined. This OT background from Hosea also explains why in Romans 9:25–26 Paul not only applies the title "beloved" to the Church, but also "my people" and "sons of the living God." The application of "beloved" along with these other titles is

---

17. Beale, *New Testament Biblical Theology*, 707.
18. Ibid.

compelling evidence that the Church is now in the blessed position of receiving God's covenantal love as the new Israel.[19]

Foreknown

Paul also speaks of the Church as those whom God "foreknew" (προγινώσκω, 8:29). This term does not simply refer to intellectual knowing, but describes "that special taking knowledge of a person which is God's electing grace."[20] The background for this term recalls God's foreknowing of Israel and his covenantal love for them (יָדַע, Gen 18:19; Exod 33:17; 1 Sam 2:12; Psa 18:43; Prov 9:10; Jer 1:5; Hos 13:5; Amos 3:2).[21] Paul even speaks of ethnic Israel this way, as those whom God "foreknew" (Rom 11:2). It is noteworthy then, that Paul imports this idea of electing foreknowledge, which lies behind the "foundation of the People of God in Jewish tradition," and applies it to the Church.[22] Although Paul will later argue that there is still a future salvation for the nation of Israel, because God foreknew them (11:2), this salvation will not be experienced outside of the new covenant community of the Church.

---

19. Contra Peter Richardson, who argues that "Gentiles or even the church" do not inherit the position of Israel, but rather become God's people in a "universal sense" (Peter Richardson, *Israel in the Apostolic Church*, Society for New Testament Studies, 10 [London: Cambridge U.P., 1969], 215).

20. C. E. B. Cranfield, *A Critical and Exegetical Commentary on the Epistle to the Romans*, vol. 1, International Critical Commentary (London: T&T Clark International, 2004), 431.

21. Schreiner, *Romans*, 452.

22. Brendan Byrne, *Sons of God, Seed of Abraham: A Study of the Idea of the Sonship of God of All Christians in Paul against the Jewish Background*, Analecta Biblica, vol. 83 (Rome: Biblical Institute, 1979), 115.

The Family of Abraham

One of Paul's more explicit images depicting those in Christ as the new Israel is that identifying them as children of Abraham. In Romans 4:1-8, he argues that Abraham was justified by faith, apart from works. In 4:9 he refutes a common belief held by many Jews of his day: "Is this blessing then only for the circumcised, or also for the uncircumcised?" He answers this objection in 4:10-12 by stressing that Abraham was counted righteous before he was circumcised, so that he may be "the father of all who believe without being circumcised" (4:11). Therefore, Paul claims that to become a child of Abraham does not mean one must become Jewish through circumcision.[23] Rather, it is by faith that one has Abraham as his father (4:16-17).

In Romans there are two passages that further employ this imagery. First, in 2:25-29, believing Gentiles who are physically uncircumcised are reckoned circumcised and considered true Jews. Second, in 11:11-24 Paul says by faith Gentiles have been grafted into the one olive tree. By looking at these two passages it becomes evident that Paul firmly believes Christian Gentiles have been incorporated into the family of Abraham. And as true members of Abraham's family, they are members of the new Israel.

Circumcision and True Jewishness

We've already discussed the significance of circumcision as it pertained to entrance into the old covenant in chapter 3. Nonetheless, it is worth noting again that, to the Jew,

---

23. Moo, *Romans*, 267.

circumcision was of the utmost importance. According to Genesis 17:9-14, Abraham's children were to be circumcised as a sign of God's covenant. However, anyone who was not circumcised would be "cut off" from the covenant (Gen 17:14). Therefore, physical circumcision designated one as a member of God's covenant community—as other Jewish writings also testify. One example is found in the book of *Jubilees*: "And every one that is born, the flesh of whose foreskin is not circumcised on the eighth day, belongs not to the children of the covenant which the Lord made with Abraham, but to the children of destruction" (*Jub.* 15.26).[24]

In the Maccabean period, Antiochus Epiphanes decreed that the Jews should not circumcise their sons. Circumcision therefore became "a test of covenant loyalty and a mark of Jewish national distinctiveness" (1 Macc 1:48, 60-61).[25] This even led to the Hasmoneans insisting on the circumcision of foreigners who dwelt in the land (*Ant.* 13.257-58, 318). Circumcision not only marked off a person as belonging to the people of God, but some Jews believed it secured salvation and kept one from going to Gehenna.[26] As has been observed, the rite of circumcision was extremely important in Second Temple Judaism. Such views were likely still prominent during Paul's day (Acts 15:1), and he combats these beliefs in Romans 2.[27]

In Romans 2, Paul aims to demonstrate that no one outside of Christ will escape the judgment of God. He argues that if

---

24. Charles R. Henry, ed., *Pseudepigrapha of the Old Testament*, vol. 2. (Bellingham, WA: Logos Bible Software, 2004), 36.

25. Dunn, *Romans 1-8*, 119.

26. Joseph A. Fitzmyer, *Romans: A New Translation with Introduction and Commentary*, The Anchor Bible, vol. 33 (New York: Doubleday, 1993), 321.

27. Moo, *Romans*, 167.

the Jews practice the same things that the Gentiles do, they
cannot expect to find mercy from God on the last day (2:1–5).
Since God does not show partiality (2:11), he will judge each
person, whether Jew or Gentile, according to what they have
done (2:6–10). Speaking to those who call themselves Jews
(2:17), Paul wishes to remove any presumption they may have
that merely possessing the law (2:12–24) or bearing the mark
of circumcision (2:25–29) will deliver them on the day of God's
wrath (2:5, 7–9, 12, 27). As Theilman states, "Jewish sin is as
grave in God's sight as Gentile sin, and identity with Jewish
people will give no one an advantage on 'the day of wrath
when his righteous judgment will be revealed' (2:5)."[28]

In 2:25–29, Paul specifically addresses the issue of circumcision. He begins by stating that, under the new covenant,
physical circumcision has no salvific value because to accept
it would demand keeping the whole law (2:25). However, Paul
later says that "by works of the law no human being will be
justified" (3:20). Therefore, Paul definitively says to the Jew
who boasts in his circumcision, "If you break the law, your
circumcision becomes uncircumcision" (2:25). In other words,
this individual is not a member of the people of God. In 2:26,
Paul flips the scenario: "If a man who is uncircumcised keeps
the precepts of the law, will not his uncircumcision be regarded (λογισθήσεται) as circumcision?" Believing Gentiles are
being counted as children of Abraham, without bearing the
mark of physical circumcision.

How is this possible? Paul's point is that with the inauguration of the new age, true Jewishness and circumcision
are not physical (2:28); rather, they are spiritual realities

---

28. Thielman, *Theology of the New Testament*, 352.

made possible by the eschatological work of the Sprit (2:29). Therefore, Paul is not merely defining who the true ethnic Jews are.[29] On the contrary, 2:28-29 are the basis for how to regard a Gentile as "circumcised" even though he is physically uncircumcised. Paul undermines any notion that the people of God are determined by ethnicity: "The Jew is not one outwardly, neither is circumcision outward in the flesh, but the true Jew is in secret, and true circumcision is of the heart by the Spirit not the letter" (2:28-29a). Already, in 2:16, Paul told his interlocutor, "God will judge the secrets (τὰ κρυπτὰ) of men." Paul now sheds light on what the final judgment will reveal: Not all who are ethnically Jews are really Jews. The true Jews are those in secret.[30] Therefore, the fundamental aspect of Paul's antithesis is between that which is seen (2:28a) and that which is hidden (2:29a).

In light of this salvation-historical contrast, Paul can say elsewhere, "For neither circumcision counts for anything, nor uncircumcision, but a new creation" (Gal 6:15). That some Gentiles are able to "observe" and "fulfill" the law is evidence that the new age has arrived.[31] Paul will elaborate on this phenomenon in Romans 8, where he says "in Christ" the law is fulfilled in believers (8:1-4). Therefore, Paul is redefining who belongs to the people of God.[32] With the dawn of the new age, all who have been circumcised in heart are considered true

---

29. Contra Barry E. Horner, *Future Israel: Why Christian Anti-Judaism Must Be Challenged* (Nashville: B&H Academic, 2007), 278-79; Vlach, *Has the Church Replaced Israel*, 146-47. Moo correctly says, "Paul is not so much describing a group of people as specifying what it is that qualifies a person to be a 'true Jew' and so to be saved" (Moo, *Romans*, 175).

30. Cranfield, *Romans*, 1:175.

31. Schreiner, *Romans*, 143.

32. Herman Ridderbos, *Paul: An Outline of His Theology* (Grand Rapids: Eerdmans, 1997), 334.

Jews (2:29). This redefinition anticipates where, in Romans 4, Paul says that all those of faith are regarded as Abraham's children (4:11–12).

In Romans 2:25–29, Paul has effectively removed any room for boasting in Jewish nationalism. He has argued that with the coming of the new covenant, physical circumcision no longer marks one off as a member of the people of God. To rely on circumcision to render a favorable verdict at the judgment is a worthless endeavor—to do so would require perfect obedience to the Mosaic law. However, those who have been circumcised in heart are now able to "[keep] the precepts of the law" and will therefore be reckoned as circumcised on the last day. True Jewishness is not something external. Rather, it is an inward reality made possible by the work of the Holy Spirit. Again, Paul has demonstrated that being a true child of Abraham has nothing to do with ethnicity. Unlike "membership in old Israel [which] required circumcision and acceptance of the Law; membership in the new Israel requires individual personal faith and confession of Christ as Lord (Rom 10:9)."[33]

The Olive Tree

In Romans 11:16–24, Paul includes another image illustrating that Gentiles—through faith—have become members of Abraham's family: an "olive tree" (11:17) with both natural and wild branches (11:17, 21, 24). This olive tree pictures the one people of God, including both believing Jews and Gentiles. Paul's choice of the olive tree to represent the people of God

---

33. George E. Ladd, *A Theology of the New Testament* (Grand Rapids: Eerdmans, 1993), 590.

is not an accident; he borrows this imagery from the prophets, who identified Israel as an olive tree (Jer 11:16; Hosea 14:5–6).[34] Even in later Jewish literature, Israel would be described as God's planting or olive tree (2 Macc 1:29; *Jub.* 1.16; *1 Enoch* 10.16; 26.1; 84.6; 93.10; *T. Sim.* 6.2; 1QS 8.5; 11.8; 1QH 14[6].15–17; 16[8].5–11; Philo, *Sobr.* 13 §65).[35]

Within Paul's olive tree analogy, the wild branches are the Gentiles—not the Church—and the natural branches are the Jews. Note here that the Gentiles are included in the olive tree by means of Israel's rejection of the gospel (11:11–12, 15, 19). Paul's Gentile audience most likely would have assumed this inclusion, because he warns them not to think of themselves as superior to the Jews who for the most part have been "broken off" (11:17). It is possible, then, that the Gentiles overemphasized the truth that they were the new people of God, the new Israel, and believed they had even replaced Israel.[36] In order to eliminate Gentile boasting over Jews, Paul reminds them that they "now share in the nourishing root of the olive tree … it is not you who support the root, but the root that supports you" (11:17–18). The "root" that the Gentiles now share in is the patriarchs and the promises that were given to them.[37] This identification of the root is confirmed in 11:28–29: Israel is "beloved for the sake of their forefathers. For the gifts and the calling of God are irrevocable."

Therefore, as Paul's olive tree analogy shows, believing Gentiles belong "not to a new body discontinuous with Israel

---

34. Moo, *Romans*, 702; Leon Morris, *The Epistle to the Romans*, Pillar New Testament Commentary (Grand Rapids: Eerdmans, 1988), 413.

35. Schreiner, *Romans*, 605.

36. Moo, *Romans*, 704.

37. Cranfield, *Romans*, 2:567; Moo, *Romans*, 704; Schreiner, *Romans*, 600.

but to Israel itself."[38] However, this Israel is not national Israel, for unbelieving Jews are excluded. Rather, this is "the spiritual Israel within Israel that, according to Romans 9, has always been in existence and, according to 11:16, grows from the seed of God's promises to the patriarchs.[39] This olive tree, which consists of both believing Jews and Gentiles, is the Church, a continuation of spiritual Israel expressed under the new covenant. Consequently, it is appropriate then to identify this new covenant people as the new Israel.

The Family of God

To be a member of the true family of Abraham is also to be a part of the family of God. In Romans 8 Paul makes it clear that those who have received the eschatological gift of the Spirit are "sons of God" (8:14). The Holy Spirit even testifies to believers that "we are children of God" (8:16). As we saw in chapter 2 of this book, Israel was identified as being the son(s) of God (Exod 4:22; Deut 14:1; Isa 43:6; Jer 3:19; 31:9; Hos 1:10; 11:1). Therefore, with Paul's application of this title to "all who are led by the Spirit of God" (8:14), he identifies the Church as true children of God, the new Israel.

This identification is made even clearer through Paul's imagery of "adoption" (υἱοθεσία, 8:15, 23). That the term "adoption" (υἱοθεσία) is only used by Paul and is not even found in the LXX does not preclude such an idea being foreign to the Jews.[40]

---

38. Douglas J. Moo, "Paul's Universalizing Hermeneutic in Romans," *Southern Baptist Journal of Theology* 11, no. 3 (2007): 77.
39. Ibid.
40. J. M. Scott, "Adoption, Sonship," in *Dictionary of Paul and His Letters*, ed. Gerald F. Hawthorne, Ralph P. Martin, and Daniel G. Reid (Downers Grove, IL: InterVarsity Press, 1993), 16.

Paul elsewhere associates the adoption of believers with the redemption from Egypt (Gal 4:1-7), just as Israel was called out as God's son (Jer 31:9; Hos 11:1).[41] The picture of adoption is also found in 2 Samuel 7:14, where the promised Davidic king and Messiah would be like a son to God.[42]

In Romans 9:4, Paul grants the privilege of adoption as belonging to Israel. Some have tried to suggest that the adoption spoken of in Romans 9:4 is not the same adoption that Christians enjoy in Romans 8:15, 23.[43] Richard Bell goes so far to say, "The sonship or adoption which Paul speaks in 9.4 is a present possession. It is a gift which Israel has retained whether she believes in Jesus or not."[44] If Bell is correct, then why does Paul express "great sorrow and unceasing anguish" over his fellow kinsmen who are cut off from the Messiah (9:2-3)? True, the privileges of "adoption, the glory, the covenants, the giving of the law, the worship, and the promises" belong to Israel (9:4). However, the physical descendants of Abraham are not the ones who inherit theses promises; the remnant—all those who share in a faith like Abraham's—do (9:6-8; 4:16).

Furthermore, the Gentiles, through faith, are experiencing the blessed privilege of adoption that serves as the means to provoke Israel to jealousy (10:19; 11:11, 14). If the adoption that Christians share in is different than the adoption of Israel, it is unclear why Israel would become jealous; it is also more

---

41. Ibid.

42. Ibid., 17.

43. C. K. Barrett, *The Epistle to the Romans*, Rev. ed., Black's New Testament Commentaries (London: Continuum, 1991), 166; Richard H. Bell, *The Irrevocable Call of God: An Inquiry into Paul's Theology of Israel*, Wissenschaftliche Untersuchungen zum Neuen Testament, vol. 184 (Tübingen: Mohr Siebeck, 2005), 202-03.

44. Bell, *The Irrevocable Call of God*, 203.

consistent with Paul's argument in Romans to understand that all the promises of Israel are fulfilled in the Church through Christ. This truth requires Paul to address the problem of Israel's unbelief in chapters 9–11.

The issue of Israel's failure to receive God's saving promises is highlighted as one compares Romans 8 and 9.[45] In chapter 8, Christians are said to receive the "Spirit of adoption" (8:15), which anticipates their eschatological adoption (8:23). In chapter 9, adoption is the privilege which belongs to Israel (9:4). Again Christians are called "sons" and "children of God" (8:14, 16–17, 19, 21) who will be "conformed to the image of [God's] son" (8:29). Israel, on the other hand, is also called God's children (9:8), and the eschatological people of God will be called "sons of the living God" (9:26). These privileges are closely related in both chapters with God's calling (8:28, 30; 9:7, 12, 24, 25, 26), election (8:28, 33; 9:11) and glory (8:18, 21, 30; 9:4, 23).[46] Therefore, the significance of the interconnectedness between chapters 8 and 9 is that the privileged blessing of Israel has become the object of the Christian's hope.[47]

By being united to Christ, both Jews and Gentiles have received the blessing of joining God's family. As members of the household of God, believers are heirs with Christ, inheriting all the saving promises of God. That Gentiles are equal sharers in this inheritance is what Paul later calls a "mystery that was kept secret for long ages but has now been disclosed and through the prophetic writings has been made known to all nations, according to the command of the eternal God, to bring

---

45. Byrne beneficially pointed out the parallels between Romans 8 and 9 (Byrne, *Sons of God, Seed of Abraham*, 127–28).

46. Ibid., 128.

47. Ibid.

about the obedience of faith" (16:25-26). Paul's usage of "mystery" (μυστήριον) refers to something previously hidden but now revealed. The mystery to which Paul refers was not that the Gentiles would merely become members of the people of God—this could be ascertained in the OT (Gen 15:3; Exod 12:48; Pss 47:9; 87:6; Isa 11:10; 19:24-25). What was obscure in the OT was whether or not the Gentiles would be subordinate to the nation of Israel (Psa 72:10-11; Isa 2:2-4; 45:14; 49:23; 60:10-14; Mic 7:17; Zech 14:17).[48] Keeping this mystery in mind, Paul argues that, through faith in Christ, Gentiles have inherited the same promises and privileges as Israel. This is the mystery revealed through the gospel of Jesus Christ to bring about the obedience of faith among all the nations (1:1-5; 16:25-27).

Summary

Paul applies Israelite language to the Church because the OT promises are fulfilled there. As the new assembly of the Lord, the "Church," like Israel of old, has been "called" by God (Rom 1:6; cf. Isa 41:9) to be "saints" (Rom 1:7; cf. Exod 19:6); "beloved" (Rom 9:25; cf. Deut 32:15); and "foreknown" (Rom 8:29; cf. Amos 3:2). These titles had been exclusively applied the nation of Israel, but in Romans refer to the Church. Because the Church bears these titles, it is consistent for Paul to identify the Church with the family of Abraham (Rom 4:16). Through the eschatological work of the Spirit, true Jewishness is not external through physical circumcision, but rather internal by the circumcision of the heart (2:28-29). With this salvation-historical shift, Gentiles are now being grafted into

---

48. Schreiner, *Paul*, 57.

God's "olive tree" whose root is the patriarchs, thus becoming members of Abraham's family (11:16–24). Finally, as members of Abraham's family, the Church consists of those who have been adopted into the family of God and become heirs of God's promises (8:14–17). With the application of this Israelite imagery, Paul has identified the Church as the new Israel and rightful recipients of all God's promises.

CHAPTER 5

Implications for the Future of Israel in Romans 11

I f the Church is the new Israel, what, then, is the future of ethnic Israel? Does this mean the Church has replaced Israel, leaving the nation with no future? Or does a future for Israel negate the Church's place as the new Israel? Richardson, for example, contends that "as long as a part of 'Israel' is expected to come to repentance, it is unlikely that the name would be appropriated" to the Church.[1] Nevertheless, we must reject the false dichotomy that this objection includes. Rather, we may find it more helpful to consider the Church to be the new Israel while at the same time holding to a future for ethnic Israel.

---

1. Peter Richardson, *Israel in the Apostolic Church*, Society for New Testament Studies, 10 (London: Cambridge U.P., 1969), 73. See also, Barry E. Horner, *Future Israel: Why Christian Anti-Judaism Must Be Challenged* (Nashville: B&H Academic, 2007), 313–14; Michael J. Vlach, *Has the Church Replaced Israel?: A Theological Evaluation* (Nashville: B&H Academic, 2010), 193.

In Romans 9–11, Paul answers an objection: A Jewish interlocutor protested that Paul's gospel questions God's faithfulness to Israel. From what Paul has argued in Romans, ethnicity
does not determine the people of God (2:25–29). The promises
that were made to the nation of Israel are fulfilled in those
who believe in Jesus Christ, whether Jew or Gentile.[2] Those
in Christ are the children of Abraham (Rom 4), inheritors of
the promise, God's elect and adopted sons who have received
the promised Spirit (8:14–29).[3] With the dominance of Gentile
reception in Paul's gospel, coupled with the vast rejection by
the Jews, it "seems that Israel has not only been disinherited
but replaced."[4] If the Jews have been rejected, then it appears
that God's promises to Israel have failed. Therefore, God's
faithfulness is brought into question.[5]

Despite such appearances, Paul discards any notion that
God's promises to Israel have failed when he says, "It is not
as though the word of God has failed" (9:6). In order to defend the righteousness of God, Paul argues that there is still a
future for ethnic Israel (11:26). Nevertheless, how God fulfills
his promises to the nation is a mystery (11:25)—and it is this
mystery that Paul explains in 11:25–32.

Our discussion here of Israel's future will be limited to
11:25–26. In examining these two verses, we must ask: What
does Paul mean by, "And in this way all Israel will be saved"?
Scholars usually answer this question in three ways.

---

2. Douglas J. Moo, *The Epistle to the Romans*, New International Commentary on
the New Testament (Grand Rapids: Eerdmans, 1996), 549.

3. Ibid.

4. Ibid.

5. N. T. Wright, *The Climax of the Covenant: Christ and the Law in Pauline Theology*
(Minneapolis: Fortress Press, 1992), 236.

Does Israel Refer to the Church?

In response to this first question, John Calvin argued that when Paul refers to "all Israel" he is speaking of the Church, the elect among both the Jews and Gentiles. He states:

> I extend the word "Israel" to all the people of God according to this meaning – "When the Gentiles shall come in, the Jews also shall return from their defection to the obedience of faith; and thus shall be completed the salvation of the whole Israel of God, which must be gathered from both."[6]

Calvin finds support for his view in Galatians 6:16, where Paul seems to identify the Church as the "Israel of God." Although, in my opinion, Calvin rightly interprets Galatians 6:16, his understanding of Romans 11:26 is improbable; it presents the Israel in 11:25 as different from the Israel of 11:26. This is unlikely for at least two reasons. First, in 11:25 Paul says, "A partial hardening has come upon Israel, until the fullness of the Gentiles has come in." Clearly in this verse Paul speaks of ethnic Israel. Therefore, it is difficult to imagine Paul abandoning this definition of Israel without some explanation. Second, Paul is in some measure reacting to the Gentile tendency to boast over the Jews (11:18), who view themselves as exclusive heirs of the promise.[7] To suggest, as Calvin does, that the Israel being saved is the "new Israel" would not serve as a correction to the Gentiles.

---

6. John Calvin, *Commentaries on the Epistle of Paul the Apostle to the Romans*, trans. John Owen, Calvin's Commentaries (Grand Rapids: Baker Books, 2009), 437.
7. Ibid.

Does Israel Refer to Elect Jews?

The second view understands "Israel" to refer to the nation; however, the salvation Paul mentions is not an eschatological one but rather refers to the salvation of elect Jews throughout all of history. Scholars who hold this position include Herman Ridderbos, O. Palmer Robertson, and N. T. Wright.[8] Several reasons support why "all Israel" means elect Jews throughout history. First, the whole context of Romans 9–11 should come to bear on what Paul says in chapter 11. Looking to 9:6–7, Paul has already defined who Israel is: "For not all who are descended from Israel belong to Israel, and not all are children of Abraham because they are his offspring." In other words, "God's promise to Abraham never included the promise that his descendants would be saved based on their ethnic identity. True Israel consists of those who are children of the promise."[9] Thus for Paul to propose that a future salvation is in store for ethnic Israel would contradict what he said about there being no soteriological distinction between Jews and Gentiles.[10] Second, Paul's question does not relate to the future salvation of Israel, but rather pertains to whether or not God has rejected them; some argue that Paul nowhere anticipates a future salvation. On the other hand, Paul's emphasis is on the continued hope that God will save some from Israel.

---

8. Ridderbos, *Paul*, 354–61; O. Palmer Robertson, *The Israel of God: Yesterday, Today, and Tomorrow* (Phillipsburg, NJ: P&R Publishing, 2000), 187; Wright, *The Climax of the Covenant*, 231–57; Charles M. Horne, "The Meaning of the Phrase 'And Thus All Israel Will Be Saved' (Romans 11:26)," *Journal of the Evangelical Theological Society* 21, no. 4 (1978): 328–34; Ben L. Merkle, "Romans 11 and the Future of Ethnic Israel," *Journal of the Evangelical Theological Society* 43, no. 4 (2000): 707–22.

9. Merkle, "Romans 11," 712.

10. Wright, *The Climax of the Covenant*, 236.

Others offer that Paul did not envision a future salvation because his focus on a remnant (11:5). So in 11:25 when Paul mentions that a partial hardening has come upon Israel he "is speaking quantitatively ('in part') and not temporally ('for a while')."[11] Therefore, a part of Israel is hardened until the full number of the Gentiles comes in, and it is in this "manner all the elect within the community of Israel will be saved."[12] Theoretically, this understanding makes better sense of Paul's discussion of a remnant; only "a part" of Israel being saved addresses why most Jews currently reject the gospel. Otherwise, to suggest that Paul speaks of a future salvation for Israel would make his discussion on the remnant seem arbitrary.

This view is appealing and certainly more plausible than the first. Nonetheless, in the end these "proofs" are not persuasive. For starters, Paul's use of "mystery" (μυστήριον) is not adequately addressed. Merkle rightly identifies the "mystery" to be threefold: "(1) the hardening of part of Israel; (2) the coming in of the fullness of the Gentiles; and (3) the salvation of all Israel."[13] However, he does not explain how Paul's revelation of the mystery is anything new. After all, Paul has already shown that throughout history it was only the elect/remnant who were saved (11:1–5). Therefore, to assert that "all Israel" simply refers to all the elect Jews hardly classifies as a mystery. Would not such a statement be obvious?

An additional difficulty with this position is the way it handles Paul's use of "all" (πᾶς) in 11:26. If one only had 11:25–26, the argument could be made that "all" should be limited to the elect throughout history. However, the rest of Romans 11 does

---

11. Merkle, "Romans 11," 715.
12. Robertson, *The Israel of God*, 186.
13. Merkle, "Romans 11," 715.

not allow such an interpretation. Throughout Romans 11 Paul builds up to 11:26 by contrasting Israel's present rejection with her full acceptance (11:12, 15, 23–24). Because of Israel's current rejection, great blessing has come to the Gentiles. Paul therefore remarks, "How much more will their full inclusion mean!" (11:12). Paul's anticipation for Israel's acceptance is illustrated in table 1. Paul's progression of thought can be clearly understood as reaching a climax in Israel's full salvation in 11:26. Therefore, the present situation for Israel is different than what will be in the future.[14]

Table 1: Tension between Israel's Rejection and Acceptance

Israel's Current Rejection	Israel's Future Acceptance
"riches for the Gentiles" (11:12a)	"how much more will their full inclusion mean" (11:12b).
"reconciliation of the world" (11:15a)	"what will their acceptance mean but life from the dead" (11:15b).
Gentiles were "grafted ... into a cultivated olive tree" (11:24a)	"how much more will these ... be grafted back into their own olive tree" (11:24b).

Therefore, when Paul says a "partial hardening has come upon Israel" (11:25), he is referring to the present state of Israel's rejection of the gospel. This state will continue "until the fullness ($\pi\lambda\acute{\eta}\rho\omega\mu\alpha$) of the Gentiles has come in." Paul's use of "fullness" ($\pi\lambda\acute{\eta}\rho\omega\mu\alpha$) in Romans 11 serves as a clue for how

---

14. Moo, *Romans*, 723–24.

one should interpret "all" (πᾶς) in 11:26. Paul says the πλήρωμα of Israel (11:12b) will not occur until the πλήρωμα ("fullness") of the Gentiles has been consummated (11:25b). Once all the elect from among the Gentiles believe, it is at this time "all Israel will be saved" (11:26a). Consequently, the "all" (πᾶς) of 11:26a must correspond with the "full inclusion" (πλήρωμα) of 11:12b. Otherwise, Paul's argument would be anticlimactic.[15]

DOES ISRAEL REFER TO THE NATION?

That "all Israel" refers to a future salvation of the nation as a whole is the majority position held by scholars today.[16] However, this does not mean that every Israelite throughout history will be saved.[17] Besides, such an assertion runs contrary to the heart of Romans (cf. 2:3–4). All those Israelites who have been hardened and die in this state will receive judgment from God. As Schreiner says:

> The point of 11:11–32 is that this hardening of Israel will not last forever. At the conclusion of history God will remove their hardness and the end-time generation of ethnic Israel will be

15. Cranfield, *Romans*, 2:577; contra Wright, *The Climax of the Covenant*, 250.
16. Cranfield, *Romans*, 2:577; C. K. Barrett, *The Epistle to the Romans*, Rev. ed., Black's New Testament Commentaries (London: Continuum, 1991), 207; Craig A. Blaising, "The Future Of Israel As A Theological Question," *Journal of the Evangelical Theological Society* 44, no. 3 (2001): 450; George E. Ladd, *A Theology of the New Testament* (Grand Rapids: Eerdmans, 1993), 606–08; Moo, *Romans*, 723; Kim Riddlebarger, *A Case for Amillennialism: Understanding the End Times* (Grand Rapids: Baker Books, 2003), 194; Schreiner, "The Church as New Israel," 29.
17. Contra Bell, who states, "If the gifts and call of God are irrevocable (Rom. 11.29), it would seem natural to take πᾶς Ἰσραὴλ in 11.26 as diachronic. ... Rom 11:26-27 suggests that Israelites from every age will believe in the Christ when they see him coming again in his glory" (Richard H. Bell, *The Irrevocable Call of God: An Inquiry into Paul's Theology of Israel*, Wissenschaftliche Untersuchungen zum Neuen Testament 184 [Tübingen: Mohr Siebeck, 2005], 265).

saved, and he will fulfill his covenantal promises. No hope, however, is held out to Israelites
who die without acknowledging Jesus as their
Messiah.[18]

Such a conclusion makes the most sense out of the context.
First, it explains how Israel's salvation is a mystery—namely,
what was not seen in the OT is that (1) a partial hardening has
presently come upon the nation of Israel; (2) this hardening will continue until the full number of the elect Gentiles
comes in; and then (3) the nation of Israel will experience an
eschatological salvation. Therefore, Israel's present condition
(11:7–10) is not her permanent condition (11:11–16). Second, for
the reasons already stated, a future salvation of the whole of
Israel adequately explains the "all" ($\pi\tilde{\alpha}\varsigma$) in 11:26.

In sum, in 11:26 Paul does not define "all Israel" to be the
new Israel. Neither does he see the "fullness" of Israel's salvation as occurring throughout history. Rather, Paul envisions
a day when the vast majority of Israel will turn to Christ and
be saved. These Israelites who embrace the true Israel, Jesus,
will then receive all the saving promises of God along with
everyone else who believes.

The Nature of Israel's Future

After arguing for a future salvation for the nation of Israel, we
should be able to clearly see that this view does not contradict
Paul's conception of the Church as the new Israel. However,
not all scholars are convinced. Eastman, for example, main-
tains that a future salvation for Israel prohibits taking the

---

18. Schreiner, *Romans*, 511–12.

name of Israel and applying it to those in Christ. She notes, "Such an identification of Israel with the church would claim a theoretical continuity with God's people, but at the cost of making *Israel* merely a cipher without reference to Paul's own people who historically claimed that name."[19] The primary difficulty with this proposal is its failure to understand Paul's view of the remnant in Romans 9–11: as a sign that God has not rejected ethnic Israel, but will one day show the nation eschatological mercy.

Beginning in 9:6, Paul states that there is an Israel within Israel, one of physical descent (9:7a, 8a) and one according to promise (9:7b, 8b). It is those Israelites who have been elected and called by God who are truly the children of God and off-spring of Abraham (9:8b, 11). For example, it was Isaac rather than Ishmael who was the child of promise, even though both were physical descendants of Abraham (9:9). At this point it could be objected that Ishmael obviously wasn't a child of promise because he was birthed by Hagar. However, the account of Jacob and Esau shows twins, descendants of Abraham and Isaac, with the same mother, yet one is a true child of God whereas the other is not. Therefore, contrary to Eastman, Paul does not simply reinforce the idea that historical Israel was determined by promise.[20] Rather, he is distinguishing a true Israel of promise within historical or ethnic Israel.

This distinction becomes more apparent as Paul expounds upon God's freedom to show mercy to whomever he wills and to harden whomever he wills (9:15–18). God's purpose of election then magnifies his mercy, which he freely gives

---

19. Eastman, "Israel and the Mercy of God," 389–90.
20. Ibid., 382.

to those whom he has called (9:24). In 9:27, then, Paul aligns himself with Isaiah, who also speaks of an Israel within Israel: "Though the number of the sons of Israel be as the sand of the sea, only a remnant of them will be saved." The reason, Paul says, that the majority of ethnic Israel will not be saved is because they have not pursued righteousness by faith (9:32). Rather, they have sought to establish their own righteousness, and have thereby rejected Jesus as their Messiah (10:3-4).

Although the word of Christ has gone out, Israel has stumbled over the rock of offense and has failed to respond to the good news of a new exodus, whereas the nations have responded positively in faith (9:30-33; 10:14-21). With this ironic turn of events, the nation of Israel has traded places with the Gentiles, who have found righteousness in Christ. In light of this "role reversal," we must ask: Has God rejected Israel? Paul answers with a resounding "No" (μὴ γένοιτο), and then presents himself as a representative of ethnic Israel who is also among the remnant (11:1-2). In other words, Paul argues that God has always preserved a remnant of Israel according to his grace (11:5).

What about the rest of national Israel? Are they forever hardened? Paul again strongly rejects such a conclusion (μὴ γένοιτο, 11:11) and proceeds to explain a "mystery" (11:25) concerning the ways of God. Paul asserts in 11:11-24 that most of ethnic Israel has been hardened and broken off from the olive tree of promise. This judgment has resulted in the salvation of the Gentiles who are being grafted into the Israel of promise. Nevertheless, Paul's point is that one day ethnic Israel, who has for the most part been hardened to the word of Christ, will be "grafted back into their own olive tree" (11:24).

Therefore, Eastman is correct to maintain that Paul anticipates a salvation of ethnic Israel at the resurrection and revelation of Christ (11:15, 26–27). Furthermore, she may also be correct in suggesting that Israel will experience God's mercy in an analogous way to Paul's encounter with the risen Christ on the road to Damascus. In this way, national Israel will be saved "by direct revelation of God's messiah apart from human preaching."[21] Nevertheless, Eastman's proposal falls short in that it fails to take into account that ethnic Israel's salvation will coincide with its becoming a part of the Israel of promise, grafted back into the olive tree along with believing Gentiles (11:17–24). This one people is the new Israel, sharing in the nourishing root of the promises of God given to Israel's forefathers (11:28).

Though we have examined the case for Paul viewing the Church as the new Israel while also maintaining a future salvation for ethnic Israel, dispensationalists still want more from Romans 11 than merely salvation for national Israel. Some advocate that Romans 11 teaches not only a future salvation for the nation of Israel, but also a future restoration.[22] Evidence for this restoration is believed to be found in Paul's appeal to Isaiah 59:20 and Jeremiah 31:33–34. Since both of these are new covenant texts, some suggest that Israel's salvation must include the "OT promises of a restoration of Israel to its land."[23] Kaiser explicitly states, "[Rom 11:27] is nothing less than a reference to the New Covenant of Jer 31:33–34, which is itself an expansion of the very promises God had made with Abraham and David. Thus, we are back to the

---

21. Ibid., 392.
22. Horner, *Future Israel*, 232–34; Vlach, *Has the Church Replaced Israel*, 161–62.
23. Vlach, *Has the Church Replaced Israel*, 162.

promise-doctrine again, which also includes the promise of the land."[24] Horner concurs, saying that "conclusive proof in this regard concerns the eschatological hope of Israel because of 'their forefathers' (Rom 11:28). Surely a reference here to the Abrahamic covenant must include the essential component of the land."[25]

Does Romans 11:26b–28 provide conclusive proof that Israel will be restored to its land? The notion of an eschatological return of Israel to prominence as a nation has several problems. First, Paul's allusion to Jeremiah 31:33–34 does not necessitate a national restoration for Israel. Paul is simply saying that Israel will not be left out of the new covenant. Further, we must not forget that the new covenant includes the Gentiles as well; otherwise, we undermine Paul's emphasis on the Gentiles being grafted into the one people of God (11:17–24).

Second, Romans 11:28 does recall God's promise to Abraham, but again Paul has already said the Gentiles are heirs of this promise (Rom 4:11–12). Furthermore, in 4:13 Paul likely sees the land promise to be expanded from Palestine to "the world." However, for the sake of argument, even if Paul did have the land promises in mind, the Gentiles would have the same right to it as the Jews. Third, the focus of these OT quotations is on God's graciousness in forgiving Israel's sins. Paul even relates this graciousness back to the Gentiles to show that Israel will receive the same mercy (11:30–31).

Therefore, Paul's objective in recalling the new covenant and God's promise to Abraham is to ground his assertion that

---

24. Walter C. Kaiser, Jr., "Kingdom Promises as Spiritual and National," in *Continuity and Discontinuity: Perspectives on the Relationship Between the Old and New Testaments*, ed. John S. Feinberg (Wheaton, IL: Crossway Books, 1988), 302.
25. Horner, *Future Israel*, 233.

Israel will be grafted back into the covenant people. Paul has come full circle from Romans 9:6 to defend the righteousness and faithfulness of God. Cranfield is certainly correct when he says:

> It is also to be noted that there is here no trace of encouragement for any hopes entertained by Paul's Jewish contemporaries for the re-establishment of a national state in independence and political power, nor – incidentally – anything which could feasibly be interpreted as a scriptural endorsement of the modern nation-state of Israel.[26]

---

26. Cranfield, *Romans*, 2:579.

CHAPTER 6

Conclusion

In the previous five chapters, I have argued that, in Romans, Paul presents the Church as the new Israel and rightful heirs of all God's saving promises. In this letter Paul contends that there is no distinction between Jew and Gentile; both receive the gift of new creation life in Christ (1:16; 6:4, 23). Paul goes to great lengths to explain how his gospel ministry to the nations has continuity with OT promises (1:1–6). However, the means by which God has brought his promises to fulfillment was a mystery "kept secret for long ages but ... made known to all nations" (16:25–26). This mystery, now revealed, is that through faith in Jesus, Gentiles have been grafted into the olive tree of Israel, being made full members of God's covenant community (11:17). Israel is no longer confined by ethnicity, but has expanded to include people from all the nations.

For Paul, the key to unlocking this mystery is found in God's Son, Jesus (1:1–4; 16:25). Jesus is the true Israel, and by means of his resurrection from the dead he has been appointed Son of God, the covenant head over the people of God, the new Israel (1:4–7). In chapter 2 of this book, we saw that the title "son of God" was applied to the nation of Israel, who as a corporate Adam were to carry out the creation mandate, exercising dominion over the earth and functioning as God's king-priests. The same title was also used in reference to the Davidic king, who would represent and lead Israel to accomplish God's purposes. When Paul calls Jesus "God's Son," he identifies him as the promised Davidic king who embodies his people Israel to fulfill God's promises of blessing the nations and making God's presence known in all the earth. Therefore, with Jesus functioning as the covenant head, God's people are now defined by being rightly related to him.

Having been united to Jesus through faith, it is not surprising that Paul calls believers "sons of God" (8:14) and "heirs of God" (8:17). As sons of God, the Church bears the title and status of Israel as God's true humanity. Thus, the Church is in the privileged position of inheriting all the promises of God. That all the promises are in view is clear: This new Israel is said to be "fellow heirs with Christ" (8:17). This means that all that Christ has inherited as God's true Son is shared among those united to him.

Chapter 3 further demonstrated that the Church has obtained these promises, which focused on the fulfillment of the new creation in Christ. Although the promise of a new creation was made to OT Israel, Paul argues that through faith in Christ, Jew and Gentile alike are experiencing the initial fulfillment of this promise in the Church. Jesus' resurrection has marked the inauguration of Israel's eschatological restoration; his resurrection was the heart of the gospel that Paul preached, whereby salvation and redemption are made available to both Jew and Gentile. The promises of the new covenant God made with Israel—namely the gift of the Spirit, the circumcision of the heart, the fulfillment of the law, and the forgiveness of sins—are all fulfilled in the Church. Moreover, since the Church includes Gentiles, the covenant of Abraham is fulfilled as well. All these promises to Israel were anticipated to come with the new creation. It is Paul's contention that through union with Christ, the blessings of the new creation have invaded the present, and the recipients of these blessings should be viewed as the new Israel.

Because the promises of OT Israel find their fulfillment in the Church, Paul understandably applies Israelite language to the Church. In chapter 4 we examined this imagery to demonstrate that Paul indeed views the Church as the new Israel. Like Israel of old, the Church is the "assembly of the Lord" whom God has called his "saints," his "beloved," and those whom he has "foreknown." The Church makes up the family of Abraham, and so are true Jews (2:28–29). Furthermore, believing Gentiles have been grafted into God's olive tree, the true people of God (11:16–24). To be a true descendant of Abraham is also to be a true member of God's family, one of those who have the eschatological Spirit, who are "children of God" (8:16). As children, they are also heirs (8:17).

Although one could object that Paul never explicitly calls the Church the "new Israel," we shouldn't reject this theological designation. To identify the Church as the new Israel is merely to grant it a term that encompasses the truth that the Church is God's new covenant people and heirs of all his saving promises. The Church is not the replacement of Israel, but the continuation of Israel reconstituted in Christ. Therefore, Gentiles through faith in Jesus are on equal footing with believing Jews, inheriting all the promises of Abraham. Nevertheless, Paul's assertion that the Church is the new

Israel does not preclude a future salvation for the nation of Israel. Rather, the mysterious plan of God presently includes a partial hardening that has come upon the nation until the full number of Gentiles has come to faith in Jesus. With the inclusion of believing Gentiles into the covenant people, God is provoking Israel to jealousy (11:11). When the salvation of the nations is completed, there will be an eschatological salvation for the whole of ethnic Israel, whereby through faith in Christ, it will be grafted back into the olive tree (11:25–26).

Paul envisions all those grafted into the olive tree to constitute the new Israel in Christ. As a result all the promises of God are fulfilled, and God's righteousness is upheld. Therefore, Paul can maintain that his gospel is in continuity with the OT, and he is right to take this message where Christ's gospel has not yet been heard (15:20). In light of this glorious gospel, believers should praise God for adopting them as his sons—saying along with Paul, "Oh, the depth of the riches and wisdom and knowledge of God! How unsearchable are his judgments and how inscrutable his ways!" (11:33).

SUBJECT AND AUTHOR INDEX

SCRIPTURE INDEX

Old Testament

Apocrypha and Pseudepigrapha

Other Ancient Texts